Museum of the Opera
del Duomo
of Florence

Monica Preti

# Museum of the Opera del Duomo of Florence

Electa

Translation
*Deborah Hodges*

Photographs
*Alinari*
*Bruno Balestrini*
*Massimo Listri*
*Scala*
*Paolo Tosi*

The Museum of the Opera del Duomo was inaugurated on the 3rd May 1891. The premises underwent complete renovation for the occasion: in the first half of the fifteenth century they had become the offices of the Magistratura dell'Opera, an organization created at the end of the thirteenth century to supervise the construction of the new Cathedral and permanently sponsored by the Arte della Lana (the Wool Guild) from 1331, adopting the Guild's emblem of the Agnus Dei (with the addition of the word OPA, the crossed P being an abbreviation of PER). The structure of the original building by Filippo Brunelleschi in 1432 is no longer visible, but the majolica (two reliefs and the *Agnus Dei*) by della Robbia, which formed part of the decoration, is conserved in the entrance hall.

For many centuries, the offices of the Magistratura also served as a temporary deposit for sculptures: these were either awaiting a location within the Cathedral, or had been removed due to a change in contemporary taste and subsequently were to be sold, placed elsewhere or permanently set aside. Two resounding examples of this process were the dismantling of the original facade by Arnolfo di Cambio in 1587 and the removal of the two famous choir galleries («cantorie») by Donatello and Luca di Robbia in 1688. Although the collection which took form in these offices was undoubtedly inconsistent, empirical and lacking organic unity, it was usually mentioned in guides to Florence from the seventeenth to the nineteenth centuries as both remarkable and singular.

The idea of a Museum dell'Opera took concrete form during the nineteenth century, when fifteenth century sculpture was re-evaluated both from an artistic and historiographic point of view, and a positivist approach was taken towards the important collection of the Opera.

One of the first to apprehend this changed cultural standpoint was Giovanni degli Alessandri, Deputy for the Opera del Duomo, and at the same time, Director of the Florentine Galleries. He appreciated the true artistic value of the two choir galleries (at that time still dismantled) and of other sculptures in the offices of the Opera and had them transferred to the Uffizi in 1822.

In the same year, degli Alessandri commissioned a young architect, Giovan Battista Silvestri, to study a project for a facade which would conform in style with the oldest part of the Cathedral. A long series of nineteenth-century projects for the facade led to the approval of that of Emilio de Fabris in 1871; the result of his meticulous historical and archaeological study of the remaining original structure. The consequent recovery of documentary material relative to the artistic history of the Cathedral was a decisive factor in the re-appraisal of the Opera del Duomo collection. It was not by chance that the architect who completed the new facade in 1887, Luigi Del Moro, had already proposed in 1885 to restructure the offices of the Opera, thus providing space for the Museum.

The idea of a Museum was principally instigated by the necessity to find a suitable location within the offices of the Opera for the two choir galleries, which had been transferred from the Uffizi to the Bargello in 1870. Certainly within the general scheme of the works and studies related to the Cathedral, however, the creation of a permanent and organic museum also came to have a symbolic and commemorative value.

There were a number of important works of art, apart from the choir galleries, already to be found in the museum at its inauguration. Following the fusion of the Opera di San Giovanni with that of the Duomo, the analogous collection relating to the Baptistry had been amalgamated with that of the Cathedral. Other important works of art (including reliefs and fragments from the Choir by Baccio Bandinelli) had been deposited in the Opera subsequent to the overall restoration of the Cathedral in 1842.

The collection, (described in the accurate, anonymous catalogue printed in 1891 and attributed to Umberto Rossi) had not yet been clearly and organically arranged in the museum and was to undergo a series of transformations, alterations and amplifications over the following decades.

Any definitive project for the museum display had to be subordinated firstly to the results of archaeological and historical research and secondly, to the varying necessities of conservation and restoration. There has indeed been a large amount of research activity and recovery of lost works since the beginning of the twentieth century.

To mention but a few of the most important examples: panels belonging to the original baptism font of the Baptistry were rediscovered in 1905 and this led to its reconstruction and the removal of the baroque altar by Ticciati; from 1897 onwards, numerous statues belonging to the Arnolfian facade were located in palaces and gardens all over Florence and this resulted in the transformation in 1937 of one of the two Brunelleschi courtyards into a new room, entirely dedicated to these.

Following the closure of the Museum during the

*Andrea della Robbia, the Eternal Father*
*between two angels.*

war (1940-1948), the new vigilant and interventionist policy of conservation led to the inclusion in the Museum of works of art taken from the Cathedral, the Bell Tower and the Bapistry; these were often replaced by plaster casts *in loco*.

The sixteen statues from the Bell Tower were transferred to the Museum in 1948, and in 1954 two new rooms to display the treasures and illuminated choral books belonging to the Cathedral were opened. Between 1965 and 1967 the panels from the Bell Tower were placed in a small room in existence since 1931.

These were the years in which the disastrous flooding of the Arno (1966) dramatically added to the damage due to atmospheric agents, severely ruining a large part of the collection already in the Museum (amongst the works suffering most damage was the Cathedral's precious collection of illuminated choral books).

The subsequent arrangement of the Museum, involving a large amount of restoration, resulted, more or less, in its present state. This is described in the precise, scholarly catalogue by Luisa Becheruc-

ci and Giulia Brunetti (1969-1970)[1]. Three major works have been added to the collection in recent years: the *Maddalena* by Donatello (1972), the *Pietà* by Michelangelo (1981) and Ghiberti's two reliefs for the Porta del Paradiso (1985). Furthermore two rooms were dedicated to the design and erection of the Cathedral's cupola on occasion of Brunelleschi's centennial (1977).

At present the collection is coherently structured but lack of space has led to its imminent expansion (and eventual reinstallation of the material). The collection is divided as follows: documentation related to the history of the Cathedral's facade, the construction of the cupola and the treasures and miniatures from the Cathedral and the Baptistry are to be found on the ground floor; the *Pietà* by Michelangelo has an isolated position on the mezzanine; sculptural works taken from the Bell Tower, the choir galleries, paintings from inside the Cathedral and works originally in the Baptistry, including the altar frontal, the silver cross, the liturgical vestments and the golden panels by Ghiberti are all on the first floor.

*Andrea della Robbia, Agnus Dei.*

10

The collection of the Museum of the Opera del Duomo represents a faithful and articulate testimony to centuries of artistic activity surrounding three major monuments of the Florentine church; centres of the city's civil and religious life and symbols of its economic and cultural vitality.

[1] This guide is mainly based on the catalogue by Becherucci and Brunetti, from which attributions and dates have been taken unless otherwise stated. For revised information, I have been greatly helped by Prof. Salvatore di Pasquale, Dott. Enrica Neri, Prof. Vincenzo Sabatino and by the Director of the Archives of the Opera, Enzo Settesoldi.

## 1. The Entrance

The entrance to the Museum of the Opera del Duomo is to be found behind the Cathedral, at No. 9. It is surmounted by a *marble bust of the Granduke Cosimo I* (1519-1574) by the Florentine sculptor, Giovanni Bandini, called «dell'Opera» because of his longterm dedication to the Cathedral works. In 1572 the bust was placed within the oval niche in an ornate frame, decorated with cartouches, wreaths of fruit and the Medici coat-of-arms. Below the bust, the insignia of the Knightly Order of the Toson d'Oro (the Golden Fleece) hanging from a collar is held by a leonine mask. Above the niche, two putti support the grand-ducal coronet. The inscription reads «Cosmus Medices Magnus D. Etruriae» (on the frame) and «Studium donavit Pius V P.M. O B» (on the border of the coronet).

On the facade of the building, to the right, a *stone tondo with the Agnus Dei*, emblem of the Wool Guild (and of the Opera) which supervised the Cathedral works.

To the left, a *marble plaque* commemorating the historian Cesare Guasti (1822-1889), who, inspired by the fin-siècle positivist spirit, was amongst the first to undertake a systematic study of the Cathedral Works' archive and this resulted in his pioneering study of Santa Maria del Fiore (1887).

The inscription reads thus: "Cesare Guasti, archivist and historian of the Cathedral Works, lived in these buildings of the Opera, which commemorates him today, from 1853 to his death in 1889. Here, in the shadow of that wonderful temple, he wrote those works, for which his name is dear to Italy 1897".

Further on, a *coat-of-arms* in stone with a three-runged ladder (14th century?) of the Falconieri family, former owners of the houses behind the Cathedral.

## 2. The Lobby

The lobby is decorated with *eight white marble columns* with carved capitals of differing designs (late 15th century) along the walls. These were removed from the Cathedral choir in 1842.

On the wall above these, a latin epigraph commemorates the founding of the Museum of the Opera del Duomo. The inscription reads thus:

"The secular deputation of the Office of Works of S. Maria del Fiore, having found the original supports of the choir galleries by Donatello and Luca della Robbia and having recovered the figurative parts through the diligence of the architect,

Emilio de Fabris, and the incessant solicitude of the deputees, who were, from 1883 to 1890; Felice Francolini, President, Tommaso Corsini, Lorenzo Strozzi-Alamanni, Pietro Torrigiani, Carlo Ridolfi, Francesco Guicciardini, caused this Museum to be built by the skill of the architect, Luigi del Moro, in order to display those marvellous works of art, now restored to their former beauty and subject of universal admiration. The year 1891".

## 3. The Courtyard

The lobby leads into a courtyard with statues and fragments from the Cathedral and Baptistry.

To the right and left of the archway, two large heraldic lions in marble bearing, to the right, the Florentine People's Cross and the date 1525 (corresponding to the style of both) and to the left, the coat-of-arms of the Opera del Duomo with the abbreviated inscription OPA. These originally formed part of the decoration of the Old Rectory, demolished in 1824.

The bases in variegated marble (discovered in the Seravezza mines in 1566) have a separate provenance; they were removed from the intercolumniation of the choir of the Cathedral.

12

On the wall to the left, apart from the marble *coat-of-arms* with the effigy of San Demetrio (17th century?) and, above it, the *head of a cherub* in marble (15th century?), there are *two columned sarcophagi* of Roman origin, copies of examples from Asia Minor, dating to the end of the 2nd century B.C.

The iconography of both relates to public life. The first, with a lid decorated with laurel leaves, has five niches in high relief between spiral columns on the front: the matrimonial ceremony (the «dextrarum junctio») is portrayed in the centre, the bride with a veil over her hair and the bridegroom in civil clothes. The couple reappear in the niches to each side of this, the military uniform of the man indicates his double role. At the far sides, Casto and Pollux, symbols of eternity. The ends of the sarcophagus are decorated with low reliefs of a «vittimario» with a bull (on the right) and the presentation of a barbarian prisoner to an emperor (on the left).

The second sarcophagus has three niches on the front divided by fluted columns: in the centre, the Gate of Hades (a popular iconographical version) from which appears Mercury, guide to the dead. Next to this, two victories standing on globes and supporting trophies. In the two lateral niches, the defunct husband and wife: on the right, the man in a toga with the figure of a small son and a casket on wheels and on the left, the woman with veiled hair with a peacock and a flower. The ends of the sarcophagus are decorated with seated gryphons. The lid is not the original one, the latter having been lost during the flood of 1966. These sarcophagi came from the south side of the Baptistry and were transferred to the Museum in 1971.

The *marble shell* between the two sarcophagi originally decorated one of the buttresses of the cupola's lantern.

It has been much restored following lightening damage (Settesoldi). Next to this, a *fragment of spiral column*, Florentine, dating to the 14th century.

*Roman sarcophagus, late 2nd century B.C.*

Following the wall leading to the Museum itself, two barbarian *sarcophagi* dating to the 8th century (?), probably discovered during excavations in the Baptistry area; a *marble plaque* also dating to the 8th century with the following inscription in gothic characters: «BAPTIZATI ESTIS CRISMA PERUNCTI ESTIS/HISOPO EMUNDATI AD FONTES VIVOS RENATI/FIRMATE CORDA VESTRA UT CRESCA FIDES VESTRA/IN IPSO PERMANETE SEMPER DEUM TIMETE/EX EGIPTO VENERUNT QUI MARE TRANSIERUNT/VIRTUTES COGNOVERUNT ET LAUDES CANTAVERUNT/GLORIA TIBI CHRISTE QUI SEDES-AC BENIGNE MISERERE NOBIS QUIA PASUS ES/ET TU JORDANIS QUIA CONVERSUS EST RETRORSUM PRO NOBIS». This is traditionally considered to have come from the Baptistry. At the sides of the Museum entrance, *fragments of three spiral columns*, Florentine, dating to the 14th century.

On the right hand wall, the large marble group of *Saint John the Baptist ascending to glory with two angels*, flanked by *two candelabra in the form of angels*, by Girolamo Ticciati. In 1732 these were placed on the new high altar of the Baptistry of San Giovanni, constructed, together with the new Choir, again by Ticciati. Even though the decorative group is a fine example of Florentine baroque, renewed critical awareness concerning the original equilibrium of the Baptistry's interior led to its removal in 1912 and, as yet, no suitable location has been found (other parts of the same group are to be found in the depository of the Opera).

On the wall, a *bronze bust of the architect Luigi del Moro* (1845-'97), who was responsible for the completion of the facade of the Cathedral designed by De Fabris and, at the same time, designed and realized the original nucleus of the actual Museum of the Opera.

The inscription in his memory reads: "Luigi del Moro, architect of the Opera from 1883 to 1897 and illustrious pupil of Emilio de' Fabris, added his name with merit to the facade of the Museum of Santa Maria del Fiore, 23rd June 1902". The bust is by the sculptress, Ida Gelli, and the architectural

design by Giuseppe Castellucci. At the far end of the walls, *two leonine masks* in marble high-relief by Baccio d'Agnolo originally decorating the frieze under the external balustrade at the base of the cupola (Settesoldi).

This was only realized on one side (it can still be seen today) between 1508 and 1512; it was not continued, tradition maintains, due to Michelangelo's criticisms (who gave it the famous description of a "cricket's cage"). Above the entrance to the Museum, the *coat-of-arms of Cardinal Leopoldo de' Medici* (1617-'75) between two *Agnus Dei*, symbol of the Wool Guild and the Opera with the initials OPA in the centre and below, the inscription: "Videbunt iusti et laetabuntur"; the door leads to the vestibule.

### 4. The Vestibule

This small room, at present containing the Museum bookshop, retains some of the original decoration from the old Residenza del Magistrato dell'Opera. These are precious works in glazed terracotta by Andrea della Robbia or by his workshop: the *tondo with the Agnus Dei* (crest of the Opera and of the Wool Guild) and the lunettes above the side doors representing, on the left, the *Eternal Father between two Angels*, a particularly interesting della Robbia piece with a flat surface, and on the right, the *Madonna and Child between Two Angels* (1489).

A niche in the wall facing the entrance contains a *marble bust of Filippo Brunelleschi* in full relief and dating to the sixteenth century, perhaps based on the artist's death mask (exhibited in the Brunelleschi rooms). Although the attribution of the bust is uncertain, the niche is undoubtedly by Giovanni Bandini. It is in variegated Seravezza marble (which he also used for the Cathedral choir) and bears the inscription: PHILIPPI BRUNELLESCHI FLORENTINI ARCHITECTI CELEBERRIMI EFFIGIES OB.AN. SAL. 1444». The date of his death is incorrect.

*15 marble bas-reliefs with nudes, prophets and apostles* (in five groups) are placed along the walls. These come from the enclosure of the Cathedral choir by Baccio Bandinelli and Giovanni Bandini.

15

Bandinelli (with the collaboration of Baccio d'Agnolo for the architectural sections) was commissioned
by the Granduke Cosimo I to design the choir in its
definitive marble version, which was begun in 1547
and completed in 1572. This concluded the long,
drawn-out construction of the important architectural internal structure, begun in the fifteenth century
by Brunelleschi (who, it appears, wished it to be
octagonal in shape and positioned in the central
space under the cupola) and continued throughout
the century with a series of different projects,
including those of Donatello and Andrea del Verrocchio. Following the overall restoration of the
Cathedral's interior (1842), the choir was reduced
to its present state by the removal of twenty four of
the eighty eight wall reliefs (apart from the fifteen
on display, nine more are to be found in the
Museum depository), the *Pietà* and the statue of the
*Eternal Father* (now in Santa Croce) and the
colonnade (of which parts are in the Museum.

These bas-reliefs, considered to be amongst Bandinelli's finest works, are free from academic classicism and reveal an unusual similarity to the work of
Rosso in their «bizarre and almost ironic streak»
(Heikamp), of Bronzino and of Andrea del Sarto,
above all in their delicate chiaroscuro. The artist
who continued the panels after Giovanni Bandini's
death is not clearly identifiable but we can assume
that Bandinelli's style was carefully imitated, probably by using his drawings.
By crossing a hall containing various marble fragments (see below), we reach the Room of the
Cathedral Facade.

## 5. The Room of the Cathedral Facade

The room, opened in 1937, contains the works of
art, which survived the demolition of the unfinished
facade of Santa Maria del Fiore in 1587.
The original facade of the Cathedral of Florence
(the present facade being nineteenth century) was
conceived by Arnolfo di Cambio, an architect and
sculptor from Colle Val d'Elsa. In 1296 he began to
construct the new Cathedral dedicated to Santa
Maria del Fiore on the site of the older, and smaller,
Cathedral of Santa Maria Reparata. The new
Cathedral was to proudly reflect the increased
political and economic power of its city. Arnolfo
only erected the facade to half its height and a part
of the sides of his general plan, which was smaller
but very similar to the actual plan and already
included the cupola. At the same time the polychrome marble and mosaic facing was realized,
together with the splendid sculptural decoration.

*Baccio Bandinelli and Giovanni dell'Opera,
reliefs for the choir enclosure.*

*Baccio Bandinelli and Giovanni dell'Opera,
relief for the choir enclosure, detail.*

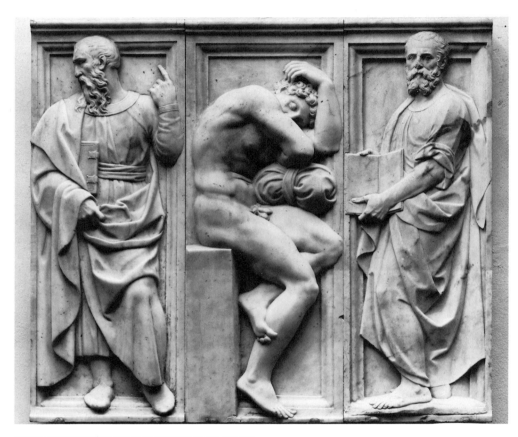

Arnolfo's design for the facade can be largely reconstructed on the basis of figurative records, above all a drawing dating from the year of its destruction (see below), and a written account of the demolition itself. The design had an original stylistic character, reflecting Arnolfo's experiences in Rome and in the Kingdom of Naples, where he had not only directly studied classical culture but, having worked for Charles I d'Angiò, had also been influenced by tendencies from the North.

Whereas Gothic architecture was the influencing factor throughout the rest of Europe, Arnolfo designed a classical facade, expressed through its proportions and the slow, scanned rhythm both of the horizontal division and of the three great portals; the larger of the three crowned with a trilobate niche and the two smaller ones surmounted by canopies, inspired by Roman ciboria. Elaborate decorative sculpture, inserted into the archi-

*The Room of the Cathedral Facade.*

*Bernardino Poccetti, drawing of the Arnolfian
facade in 1587.*

tectural structure of the lunettes, the splays and the series of niches (a typically Northern feature), developed the theme of the celebration of Mary, after whom the new Cathedral had been named.

The plasticity of the statues and the architectural framework were emphasized by the rich, chromatic effects of the multi-coloured marble, following the example of the nearby Baptistry (pink marble from the Maremma, in addition to the white and the green), and cosmatesque mosaic. Although an essential feature of the Arnolfian facade, very few traces of the original colour remain; these permit us, however, to imagine the chromatic effect of the pink background, the white marble and the glinting golden mosaic.

With the death of Arnolfo, work on the Cathedral was interrupted. His two most illustrious successors (Giotto: 1334-'37 and Andrea Pisano: 1337-'47) proceeded with the construction, after the supervision of the Cathedral works had been handed over to the Wool Guild (1331), but they turned their attention to the Bell Tower, and left unchanged the facade. Notwithstanding the nineteenth century belief to the contrary, Francesco Talenti (Master Builder from 1349 to '59), who amplified and modified the proportions of Arnolfo's project, did not superimpose a new facade. It was, therefore, Arnolfo's concept which remained the reference point for sculptors working on new material for the facade in the second half of the fourteenth and first half of the fifteenth centuries.

The facade, which had been neglected for a large part of the fifteenth century, no longer suited contemporary taste and became the subject of a competition for its renovation, which took place on 20th February 1480.

The operative decision, which at the time was prudently postponed by one of the jury, Lorenzo de Medici, was taken up without hesitation by another member of his family, the Granduke Francesco I. In 1587 he ordered the complete demolition of the facade (which took little more than five months, from 22nd January to 9th July).

An anonymous contemporary writer, in a description of this event, stated that the facade was considered «old-fashioned, with an awkward style no longer used nowadays».

Florentine historians attempted to justify the decision, describing it as a means of providing employment for citizens, impoverished after the terrible famine of 1586. It is certain, however, that foolish «modernist» pretences together with the personal ambition of Bernardo Buontalenti, a civil and military architect at the court of the Medici, led to the demolition, described with informed sagacity by the same contemporary author as a «pitiful sight». He also documented the general sentiment of the Florentine people as that of «sorrow... in witnessing the destruction of such beauty».

To the right of the entrance, a photograph of the above mentioned *drawing of the old Cathedral facade* (pen and sepia on canvas) by Bernardino Poccetti.

Bernardino Buontalenti, who bequeathed the drawing to the Opera, perhaps commissioned it from his friend and contemporary artist, in order to conserve a record of the facade before its destruction. It is considered by critics to be the most reliable source. Poccetti used it afterwards in his fresco for the first cloister of San Marco, depicting the story of Sant'Antonio.

Whereas these documents provide us with a general idea of the original architectural design and location of the various decorative elements on the Arnolfian facade, the surviving sculptures re-evoke its plastic form.

## Arnolfo di Cambio and his collaborators

On the end wall to the left, Arnolfo's statue of *Bonifacio VIII* (1294-1303) within an archway of white marble resting on violet marble (Seravezza variegated) columns and bases from the Cathedral choir. In this work, as in others linked to his name, it is difficult to evaluate the extent of his personal involvement.

Indeed, on the enormous building site of Santa Maria del Fiore, where work was organized according to the Mediaeval system of the «workshop», the Master Builder was assisted by a number of highly skilled craftsmen, reflecting the technical specialization and refined cultural level to be found in Florence at that time.

The statue of this Pope, who had contributed to the construction of Santa Maria del Fiore, was originally placed on the Cathedral facade (following the demolition of the latter, the statue was moved from one Florentine garden to another, and was finally bought by a noble descendant of Bonifacio VIII in 1893, as the inscription on the modern base testifies, who in turn presented it to the Opera. It was initially placed inside the Cathedral, and then transferred to the Museum in 1937). The arbitrary restoration dating to the seventeenth and eighteenth centuries (the reconstruction of the face, the left foot and the base, the re-arrangement of the anterior drapery between the legs and the reduction of the

20

lateral drapery, formerly in pleats, to a continuous plane) tended to support the traditional attribution to Andrea Pisano and impede the just appraisal of this great raised, seated figure, with the papal crown upon his head. Considered to be the work of Arnolfo, it is similar to the refined classicism of his Roman works and can be dated to the beginning of his work on the Florentine Cathedral, between 1296 and 1300. Immediately following this, Arnolfo began to develop the central theme of the facade, dedicated to the Virgin; the sculptures decorating the three portals, within their respective lunettes, were the *Madonna of the Nativity* (left), the *Virgin enthroned between the Saints Reparata and Zanobi* (centre) and the *Dormitio Virginis* (right). The surviving sections of this decorative scheme are displayed along the wall facing the entrance.

On the left, two extremely damaged marble *statues of prophets* from the workshop of Arnolfo di Cambio, originally on the buttresses of the left portal.

Next to these, the surviving sculptural decoration from the central portal. In the centre, majestically seated against a background of coloured marbles (green and pink with black and gold mosaic borders), the *Madonna enthroned with Child* by Arnolfo, originally from the portal lunette. The statue, object of enormous popular devotion, is one of the few to have survived the demolition of Arnolfo's facade (it was moved from the Cathedral's interior to the Opera and displayed in the Museum from its inauguration in 1891).

The iconic solemnity of this Madonna, still very close to the Byzantine typology, is given an added dimension by the plasticity of the form and the clear, synthetic, geometric conception of its volume. The concentration of expression finds its parallel in the contemporary painting of Giotto.

Flanking the Madonna, are the two original statues; *San Zanobi* (on the right), Bishop and patron of Florence, by a workshop assistant and *Santa Reparata* (on the left) by Arnolfo himself.

The latter was found in the amphitheatre of the Boboli gardens (1917), where for many centuries it had been erroneously considered an antique statue. The young palaeochristian martyr, bearing burning oil (symbol of her virginity) is stylistically close to the Madonna with Child; they represent the final and highest moment in Arnolfo's artistic activity in Florence (first decade of the fourteenth century).

Above these, there are *two curtain-bearing angels* from the workshop of Arnolfo di Cambio, which completed the decoration for the lunette of the central portal; above these, an *architrave fragment*

*Arnolfo di Cambio, Madonna with Child.*

22

with mosaic and polychrome decoration from the original facade. The *sixteen statues of Saints*, arranged in two groups of eight on each side of the *Madonna between Santa Reparata and San Zanobi*, were executed between 1387 and 1390 to decorate a similar number of niches in the splays of the same portal. They are the work of the foreign artist, Piero di Giovanni Tedesco.

High up on the wall, a marble relief of the *Madonna of the Nativity* by Arnolfo. This was acquired by the Bargello Museum from the antique trade. The reclining figure with the solemn dignity of an ancient sarcophagus has been compared to the figure of Bonifacio VIII. Its «subtly intellectual classicism» (Becherucci, in Becherucci-Brunetti) date it to the final years of the thirteenth century.

Originally inside the same lunette of the left portal and behind the Madonna, there was a mosaic panel with the figure of the Christ child and the heads of a bull and an ass (at present lost). The two beautiful *angels* by Arnolfo's workshop, which decorated the pendentives of the lunette, have been recovered.

In the original decorative scheme, the Nativity scene was flanked by figures of shepherds and animals in the adjacent niches. It is most likely that the *fragment of marble in high relief with sheep and cows*, attributed to one of Arnolfo's assistants, formed part of these.

Next to the Madonna of the Nativity, the plaster cast of the *Dormitio Virginis*, which decorated the lunette of the right portal. The original marble relief by Arnolfo di Cambio, having been transferred to Germany via the antique trade and reduced to fragments during the Second World War, has now been recomposed with the help of this cast (it is at present in the Bodemuseum, East Berlin).

The iconographic theme of the lunette of the right portal is clearly described in the document contemporary to the demolition of the facade: «The ascension of Mary, already in the grip of death, and Christ, who holds her spirit in his arms, with all the apostles surrounding the dead body».

Of this, the museum possesses only a *fragment with two heads* (above the *Dormitio Virginis*) of a bearded man and a child, which have been identified as that of Christ and of his mother's «animula»; the work of an assistant of Arnolfo.

### Sculpture for the Cathedral facade dating to the end of the fourteenth century

There was a moment of renewed activity on the Cathedral facade at the end of the 1300's. The large gallery, with the trabeated second order, was

*Arnolfo di Cambio, Madonna of the Nativity.*

decorated with the statues of four *martyr saints, Stefano, Lorenzo, Vittore, and Barnaba*, flanked by eight *adoring Angels* at the sides of the central portal. The statues remained in their original position (as one can see in the drawing by Poccetti) up until the destruction of the facade, after which event they were separated and their whereabouts not documented.

They can probably be identified as the statues to be found along the same wall facing the entrance, below the *Madonna of the Nativity* and the *Dormitio Virginis* (this identification has however been questioned).

The two headless figures represent *the Saints Vittore* (with the cloak) and *Barnaba*; they were particularly venerated by the Florentine people for the victories won on the Saints' days against the Pisans at Cascina and against the Aretini at Certomondo. The artists responsible for these statues have not been definitely identified: the first is attributed to Giovanni d'Ambrogio and the second to Nanni di Banco and represents, therefore, one of the latter's first works. They were found in the courtyard of the Palazzo Medici-Riccardi, surmounted by two antique heads, later removed when the statues were transferred to the Museum (1936).

The *Saints Lorenzo and Stefano* (flanked by an angel, bearing the stone, symbol of his martyrdom) in diaconal dress are plaster casts of the originals (in the Museum of the Louvre, Paris) by Piero di Giovanni Tedesco; the artist, who perhaps came to Florence from Milan, was active on the site of the Florentine Cathedral during the last years of the fourteenth century and brought with him the decorative and naturalistic elements of the «flowery» gothic.

He was also responsible for the series of *adoring Angels* (the one to the left of Saint Stefano is a plaster cast), which, following the destruction of the facade, finished as ornaments in a number of private and public gardens in and around Florence (Castello di Vincigliata, Villa di Castello, Boboli Gardens) before being recovered by the Museum.

Following the right hand wall, there are four rather damaged statues of the *Doctors of the Church*, again dating to the end of the fourteenth century, which decorated the third order of the facade, where they were probably situated between the niches of the pilasters. All four are documented works: *San'Agostino* and *San Gregorio* by Niccolò di Piero Lamberti and *Sant'Ambrogio* and *San Gerolamo* by Piero di Giovanni Tedesco. Transformed into the poets laureate (Homer, Virgil, Dante and Petrarch), the four statues stood at the entrance to the viale di Poggio Imperiale (already documented in the second half of the seventeenth century) and remained there until their transfer to the Museum in 1936.

### The four Evangelists

The *statues of the Evangelists* were executed between 1408 and 1415 for the two pairs of large niches flanking the central portal, and had perhaps already been included in the Arnolfian scheme. They are placed along the entrance wall: (from left to right) *San Luca* by Nanni di Banco, *San Giovanni* by Donatello, *San Matteo* by Bernardo Ciuffagni

*Nanni di Banco, San Luca.*    *Niccolò di Piero Lamberti, San Marco.*

and *San Marco* by Niccolò di Piero Lamberti.
Amongst the few statues to be salvaged after the demolition of the Cathedral facade, they were transferred to the interior of the Cathedral and later to the Museum (1936).
They illustrate the different tendencies present in one historical moment of Florentine sculpture: *San Marco* by Niccolò Lamberti is still closely linked to a late Gothic formula (the schematic linearity of the drapery and the beard, in particular), clearly contrasting with the greater naturalism and the firm relationship to the surrounding space of the sculpture of Nanni di Banco and Donatello.
*San Luca* by Nanni di Banco is a calm, proud figure: the sobre drapery emphasizes the body's form, set at a slightly oblique and withdrawn angle. The hands, firmly placed on the legs and on the book, give life to the figure, whose vital presence is emphasized by the gaze directed down towards the viewer (note that the location of these statues presupposed that the public would view them from below).
In contrast, *San Giovanni* by Donatello is characterized by a frontal, static stance with heavy, hanging hands. The abundant drapery forms heavy folds around the legs and the only slightly accented relief of the torso, when seen in profile, reveals its lack of depth. This is compensated by the strong three dimensional working of the volumes, which give a sense of profundity. The solemn and weighty impression is animated by the intensity of the facial expression with its uneasy gaze staring into the distance.
*San Matteo* by Bernardo Ciuffagni is one of this minor artist's better works: the ghibertian treatment of the drapery is superimposed on the basic formula of the San Giovanni by Donatello, which could have plausibly been copied during its creation, even though this took place in segret within the Cathedral itself. The last two statues again date to the end of the fourteenth century; the *Musician Angels* are situated in the corner, one with a portable organ and the other with a lute, and are attributed to Piero di Giovanni Tedesco. The other four angels of the same series are displayed in the adjoining passage: the *Angel with the rebeck*, both sweet and solemn, is attributed to Giovanni d'Ambrogio (more recently to Luca di Giovanni da Siena), *Angel with a bagpipe*, attributed to Lorenzo, son of Giovanni d'Ambrogio, both *Angel with a viella* and *Angel with cymbals* are attributed to Iacopo di Piero Guidi: all these artists were active at the end of the fourteenth century.

The six figures, of differing dimensions, were discovered in the garden of the Medici villa of Castello (apart from the *Angel with a rebeck*, which came from the garden of the seventeenth century palazzo della Crocetta, once property of the Medici and now the Archaeological Museum).
The date of their transfer after the destruction of the facade is unknown, but they probably formed part of its decoration, even if their precise location is unclear.
In the centre of the room, the *marble sarcophagus of the funeral monument to Captain Piero da Farnese*. Famous for his military victories at the head of the Florentine army, he conquered the Pisani at Bagno a Vena in 1363 after a strenuous battle, in which he not only lost many men but also his own steed, forcing him to ride a mule. He died of the plague in the same year at San Miniato al Tedesco.
His funeral monument, completed in 1367, was placed inside the Cathedral by order of the Republic of Florence. The equestrian statue, which originally surmounted the sarcophagus (the Captain was represented in battle dress, astride a mule, during the Battle of Bagno a Vena) appears to have been realized in wood and plaster (Follini, 1790), but is now lost.
The sarcophagus, on the other hand, was transferred to the Museum in 1936. It is an antique piece, reworked on the back and the sides with heraldic motifs. The principle side, aligned with the wall, bears the original Roman relief dating to the second century B.C., figuring the myth of Phaeton in three separate scenes, which are no longer easily distinguishable (Phaeton and Helios with the Heliades; Zeus hurls lightening at Phaeton, who falls from the Chariot of the Sun towards the waters of the Heridan; the Dioscuri subdue the horses in order to lead them back to Olympus, in the background, Phosphoros and Hesperos). This is one example of the numerous archaeological pieces to be found in Florence which, at the end of the fourteenth century, had begun to stimulate interest in the antique and led to the more complete classicism of the following century.
On the opposite side, there are three sculptured coat-of-arms: the lily of Florence, the Eagle of the Guelphs and the Cross of the People, alternated with two panels of tiny lilies. On the left end, a small shield with the Farnese lily surmonted by a leaf-shaped crest carved with a series of «M» s. On the right end, (from the base upwards) a small shield with the Farnese lily, a crest, an upturned fox

26

*Donatello, San Giovanni Evangelista, detail.*

*Etruscan (Chiusi) cippus with musicians and dancers,*
*first half of 5th century.*

(symbol of the defeated Pisans) and a small Farnese lily. The lid, leaning next to the sarcophagus, bears two crossed keys at the centre, symbol of the Papacy.

At the entrance to the next room, a fourteenth century Tuscan *holy-water basin* surmounted by a small fifteenth century *statue of an Angel with vase*. Both of these were taken from the Cathedral and replaced with copies (perhaps nineteenth century) on the original pedestal accompanying the holy-water basin.

The Angel, of a later date and of uncertain attribution (Urbano di Pietro da Cortona ?) replaced the original statue crowning the holy-water basin, which was probably damaged.

### 6. *The Passage*

The passage leading to the Brunelleschi Rooms contains other sculptural fragments from the decoration for Arnolfo's facade (to the left), and from other sources (to the right).

At the entrance, there are *two marble posts* with cosmatesque decoration from the end of the thirteenth century, discovered during the realization of the present facade.

The two headless, marble statues — *Santo Stefano* with a book and *a Prophet* with a scroll — were found, both surmounted with antique heads in the courtyard of the palazzo Medici-Riccardi together with the two statues now situated in the Room of the Cathedral Facade.

They were transferred to the Museum in about 1936 and were indentified for a long time as two of the four statues from the facade's second order, but they probably came from another part of the scheme (Becherucci, in Becherucci-Brunetti).

The first is attributed to Andrea Pisano and dated to about 1340, when he also created *the Kings* and *the Sybils* for the Bell Tower.

The second, attributed to Iacopo di Piero Guidi, is flanked by two *Musician Angels* by the same artist, already mentioned together with the other two angels flanking Santo Stefano.

The fragments include a *marble cippus* with musicians and dancers (Etruscan, first half of the fifth century) found in a cellar of the Cathedral Provostry. The other fragments displayed on the walls are Roman, second and third centuries B.C., and were used in the construction of the Bell Tower and Cathedral.

*Giovanni d'Ambrogio (?), musician angel.*

## 7. *The Brunelleschi Rooms*

Having completed the construction of the vast, powerful tambour of the Cathedral, it was necessary to resolve the problem of the «vaulting» of the enormous cupola; a problem which, although featured in Arnolfo's original project, had been continually postponed. A competition was organized and in 1420, after two years of heated discussion and many quarrels, the model presented by Filippo Brunelleschi and Lorenzo Ghiberti was chosen. It was Brunelleschi, however, who took the dominating role in the realization of the joint project by planning and resolving the multitude of technical problems which arose during the fifteen years (circa) necessary for the completion of the cupola's construction.

The problem lay in the erection of the cupola, the paradigm of which had been established many years before, during the development of the general project for the Cathedral. As its base, this cupola had an irregular octagon; contrary to the classical concept of the basilica with a circular plan, the mediaeval tradition conceived of the cupola as secondary with respect to the longitudinal development of the nave, which, therefore, conditioned its shape and size.

Brunelleschi vaulted the cupola with a pointed, ogival arch. His success lay in an original technique guaranteeing the stability of the structure without the use of a supporting framework, which would have been impossible to realize at that time. In the absence of autobiographical documents (only a «memorandum» of 1420 exists, revised and partly corrected a few years later), the only references permitting a reconstruction of Brunelleschi's technique are those which can be deduced from the structure of the cupola itself, the *De re aedificatoria* by Leon Battista Alberti (presented to Pope Niccolo V in 1452 and published in Florence in 1485 with a dedication to Agnolo Poliziano) and the *Vita di Brunelleschi* by Antonio Manetti (1423-'91) which, amongst other things, testifies to Brunelleschi's methodic study of antique monuments in Rome.

The cupola consists of a double spherical cap with a hollow space between the internal and external cupola (see below). The «fish-bone» brickwork, visible from the internal space between the two domes in the unplastered areas, is still not fully understood but is generally considered to be the means by which Brunelleschi managed to realize a structure capable of supporting itself during construction.

The construction of the cupola presented complex technical and constructive problems; it was realised with successively concentric rings, at a notable height from the ground and with no supporting framework. Brunelleschi was famous amongst his contemporaries as an ingenious inventor of machines («an admirable constructor» and gifted with «a divine genius for the invention of machines», states Marsuppini's famous epitaph in the first span of the Cathedral's right nave), and he resolved these problems by exploiting mechanical and physical principles, which were well-known but had never before been applied with such effect. The success of Brunelleschi's model was significantly ratified ten years later, around 1430, with the destruction of a brickwork model. This had been designed by eight «magistri» (artists and sculptors), approved as definite in 1367 by the Opera del Duomo, and displayed near to the Bell Tower but had never been realized.

The final ring of the cupola was completed in 1434 and the solemn consecration by Pope Eugenio IV took place on 25th March 1436. The lantern was begun immediately afterwards, following yet another much debated competition in 1436, in which Brunelleschi's model was declared winner (it was perhaps the same project which he had already presented in 1432).

The artist never saw his work completed; Vasari narrates that at his death he had realized all the various marble parts, but these were not in position until 1461.

The history of the construction of the cupola is documented in the two adjoining rooms (the display dates from 1977): the first presents models of the cupola and the second, samples of the machinery and materials used in the lengthy process of construction.

### *The cupola of Santa Maria del Fiore: the wooden models*

In the first room to the right, the *wooden model of the lantern*; the attribution to Brunelleschi is not certain. The little model (in wood with parts modelled in wax) includes the final section of the cupola with the octagonal eye of the volute formed by the converging ribs, visible in the three uncovered sails, from which rises the star-shaped lantern. This, almost identical to the actual lantern, consists of a small, windowed temple reinforced by eight buttresses and surmounted by a large frame, above which a round of blind arches sustain the small cone («pergamena») culminating in the sphere and the cross.

The date 1673 engraved on the lantern and the inaccessibility of this culminating sphere, to which Vasari refers, has thrown doubts on the authenticity of this model as the one presented by Brunelleschi in the competition of 1436 (a theory supported by Sanpaolesi, who sees greater harmony in the model than in the lantern itself, which was finished after the death of the artist). The other convincing hypothesis, presented both on the basis of documents and stylistic analysis, is that the model is a seventeenth century copy on a reduced scale, realized for a study of the statics of the building, which was continually threatened by lightening (Becherucci, in Becherucci-Brunetti). It is also possible that the lower part of the cap is original (Settesoldi, verbal communication).

Next to this, another *wooden model* , which has been in the possession of the Opera *ab antico*. Until recently it was considered to be a composition of parts of different models of the Cathedral — cupola, tambour and exedra. It was only after the flood (1966) that it was assembled in its present state and proved to be a single model of the whole Cathedral.

Notwithstanding its poor state of conservation and its fragmentary condition, which do little for its aesthetic appearance, the age of this model makes it of great importance. Although of indifferent quality, it provides a comprehensive vision of the architectural whole without detailed description of the minutiae. The tambour has sides of irregular lengths (as in the actual tambour), corresponding to the slight «irregularity» of the cupola above it. Certain features would suggest that it was made before the tambour was given its marble covering (begun in 1465): the corner pilasters are of the same width from the bottom to the top of the tambour (differing from those of the marble covering, which are narrower at the height of the first balustrade), the external ring of the tambour (differing from those of the marble covering, which are narrower at the height of the first balustrade), the external ring of the splays and the diameter of the eye openings are inferior to those subsequently realized.

It has been suggested (Marchini, 1980) that this model was made by Brunelleschi himself (in 1429?) — the tambour and exedra can perhaps be traced back to a still earlier date (to the project of the «magistri» of 1367) — in order to have an overall idea of the architectural structure at a moment when the cupola was almost completed, and the lantern was under consideration. This is followed

*Filippo Brunelleschi (?), wooden model for the Cathedral lantern.*

by a glass display case containing the *death mask of Filippo Brunelleschi* (white plaster) a copy taken from the original death mask itself. It is considered to be the model for the bust of Brunelleschi (to be found in the first span of the right nave of Santa Maria del Fiore) by his pupil and heir, Andrea di Lazzaro Cavalcanti, called il Buggiano.

The following *model of the cupola* is modern, by Natale Diana (1975) and is in wood with a metal framework, covered with coloured card (scale 1:200 circa). The section of the cupola clearly demonstrates the double spherical cap: the thicker, internal cupola has a mainly structural functional, whereas the external brick cupola serves as a protection for the former. The hollow space running between the two contains the stairway leading to the lantern, illuminated by light from the small windows in the external cap at varying levels.

The uncovered section of the cupola clearly shows the structure of the connecting arches between the external and internal cupola: the corner ribs and the two intermediary ribs are connected by small transversal arches. Recent studies have shown that the small connecting arches rest on conical, and not pyramidal surfaces (as in Diana's model). Further down, near the base of the cupola, the «centina» can be seen running around the entire circumference. Inside, the two galleries of the tambour link the cupola to the rest of the building; small windows provide illumination from the base of the spherical cap which, according to Brunelleschi's intentions (as related by his biographer, Manetti), should have been decorated with mosaic. Instead, it was entirely covered with a grandiose fresco of the Last Judgement, begun by Vasari (1572-'74) and continued by Federico Zuccari (1578-'79) with much workshop participation, resulting in a distortion of the original concept.

## The cupola of Santa Maria del Fiore: machines and materials

The connecting room contains a collection of materials and instruments relating to the construction of the cupola. For the most part, these can be dated to later than the construction itself and were used for maintenance work. They were probably based on models, designed and used by Brunelleschi. The wooden hoisting tackle (see below) is perhaps original, but even so, this alone cannot begin to illustrate the vast range and ingenious nature of Brunelleschi's technical inventions. Ample documentation of his innumerable machines exists in Leonardo da Vinci's Codice Atlantico, in the man-

uscript by Bonaccorso Ghiberti (discovered by Ladislao Reti), grandson of the more famous Lorenzo and young apprentice on the Cathedral site, and in the many drawings by Antonio da Sangallo il Giovane, who made careful studies of Brunelleschi's inventions.

In a clockwise direction: some of the *brick forms* used for the construction of the cupola, including those special bricks with an angle of 135°, corresponding to the angle of the sides of an octagon. *Two winches*, one (bearing the initials OPA and the date 1705) for the movement of materials along a horizontal surface, and the other for the vertical movement of materials. Displayed on an inclined surface, *a wooden loadbearing cart* for the transport of materials along the sails of the external spherical cap. Finally, *three hemp ropes* of various lengths (242, 218 and 203 metres).

Above the ropes, on the entrance wall: a *double pulley* in wood with cords in canvas and leather. Beyond the door, a *set square and two compasses* in metal. Along the left wall, a series of *wooden pulleys* which, by means of a system of circular levers, or small rings, demultiplacate the weight to be lifted. On the wall facing the entrance, *two iron turnbuckles*, the first with a bronze female thread and the second with a bronze ring and iron *tongs*; these instruments were used for the transport and use of construction materials. Further up the wall, in a line, *a series of iron lewis'* of varying dimensions, in two and three parts. On the extreme right of this wall and on the right wall, there is a series of *pulleys* in metal (some with the female thread in bronze) and in wood. Turning back through the Cathedral Facade Room and entering a door surmounted by the upper part of a three-mullioned window from the Bell Tower (workshop of Francesco Talenti), we reach the Room of the Choral Books.

## 8. The Room of the Choral Books

The Cathedral's important collection of Choral Books, displayed in this room, was first opened to the public in 1954. Important examples of the minor arts and wooden models of the Cathedral's facade are also on display here, following their restoration after damage incurred during the flood of 1966.

### Wooden models of the Cathedral facade

The wooden models displayed along the walls of this room (five of the seven models were conserved *ab antico* in the Guardaroba of the Opera del

Duomo) are the work of various architects from the end of the sixteenth century, at the time of the Grandukes Francesco I and Ferdinando I de Medici, to the beginning of the seventeenth century, at the time of Granduke Ferdinando II de Medici; not one of these projects was realised.

On the right of the entrance to the room, a group of the oldest models, dating to the competition following the demolition of the original facade in 1587. The clear similarity between the models in terms of their compositive structure and their stylistic characteristics, influenced by Michelangelesque architecture, has rendered their attribution very difficult, and this problem has not yet been resolved.

Only one model (it is the first on the right) has been given the universally acceptable attribution to Bernardo Buontalenti. Traditionally known as the *«modello grande»*, with a maximum measurement of 2 metres, it is the only sixteenth century model with three orders: the lower one is corinthian, the other two composite with a progressive reduction of the loadbearing structures. Buontalenti, who was First Architect and Engineer to the Medicean Court, never realized his project for the facade, due to the premature death of the Granduke Francesco I, by whom he was much favoured.

The *«modello mezzano»* (145 × 120 cm.), with two orders, the first corinthian and the second composite, has recently been attributed to Giovanni Antonio Dosio but more recently to Cigoli (for this, and other attributions: Matteoli). Its decorative characteristics create a particular harmony: the columns of Tuscanic order framing the doors, the two pairs of flaming vases above the lateral windows, the repeated motif of the banisters. The long balcony separating the two orders might perhaps have been the location for a series of statues.

The following *«modello grande»* is perhaps the work of Giovanni de' Medici (1566-1621) rather than Giambologna. It is also of two orders, the lower one corinthian and the upper one composite, and it is characterised by an almost flat treatment of the surfaces and a rigid symmetry of the architectural elements.

The *last model (grande)* of this series has two orders, the first corinthian and the second composite. Its most particular feature, however, is the large Medicean coat-of-arms placed in evidence over the central window. For this reason, it has been attributed to Giovanni de' Medici, but it is, in fact, by Giovanni Antonio Dosio. Dosio's model was proposed again in 1633 by the Granduke Ferdinand II, but the use of only two orders was not accepted.

The definitive idea of adopting a facade with three orders, considered more suitable for a monument of such importance and position, was confirmed at this time.

On the left wall, the *«modello grande»* by the Accademia del Disegno (work of various artists, headed by Giovan Battista Pieratti, who was the Superintendent of the Accademia). Following a competition won by this model, construction work began on the facade on 22nd October 1636 (when the first stone was laid). Immediately afterwards bitter differences arose between the Opera's architect, Gherardo Silvani (responsible for another model for the facade), entrusted with the realisation of the project, and Giovan Battista Pieratti whose role, as sculptor, was mainly to assist and supervise the decorative works. This forced the Granduke Ferdinando II to call a definite halt to the construction work, which had only just begun (5th November 1636).

The common concept in all these projects is the recognition of a contemporary architectural style and not the «gothicity» of the Cathedral. The actual facade was conceived from a very different standpoint: it was constructed, after a series of complications and further competitions, between 1871 and 1886, on the basis of a design by Emilio de Fabris and reflects contemporary historical romanticism. It was inspired by the oldest part of the Cathedral facade, but when the two are compared, it appears cold and overladen with minute, decorative detail.

*The illuminated Choral Books*

In the long display case against the wall facing the entrance, there are four illuminated choral books. Three of these are works saved from the flood of 4th November 1966, which ruined the important collection of Cathedral choral books already housed in the Museum, plus one of the many books restored since then.

The collection included fifty eight manuscripts, covering the entire liturgical year, not just for daily use but for special religious occasions. They were Antiphonaries, Graduals and Evangeliaries dating from the end of the fifteenth and the first half of the sixteenth centuries and had been compiled with the traditional gothic script *textualis* and musically annotated with the ancient method of the Gregorian chant.

The manuscripts are magnificently illuminated. The principal pages include large scenes incorporated into the capital letters, works by major contemporary artists: Francesco d'Antonio del Chier-

*Giovanni de' Medici model of a facade
for S. Maria del Fiore.*

*Giovanni Antonio Dosio, model of a facade
for S. Maria del Fiore.*

*Cigoli, model of a facade for S. Maria del Fiore.*

*Academy of Design, model of a facade for S. Maria
del Fiore.*

ico, Attavante degli Attavanti, Gherardo and Monte di Giovanni del Fora, Frate Eustachio and others.

From the left: *Antiphonary* (marked *D.8*), restored following damage sustained during the flood. It was decorated by Monte di Giovanni, who initially worked for illustrious private patrons (often together with his brother Gherardo), but from the last decade of the fifteenth century for the following thirty years, was involved in various projects for Santa Maria del Fiore.

From 1491 onwards he worked on the mosaic decoration for the Chapel of San Zanobi, he participated in the renovation of the Cathedral's furnishings (the painted table and the great candelabra) and, as a miniature artist, he was commissioned to illustrate various missals (the Edili 109, conserved in the Biblioteca Medicea Laurenziana and the Missal for San Giovanni in the Vatican are the only surviving examples) and a series of choral books. His miniature style is characterized by a notable variety of figurative sources, reworked in the context of contemporary iconographic tendencies and enriched by his lengthy experience as a Master of Mosaic. This is evident in his lively use of colour and the minute and regular division of his backgrounds, from which the figures stand out.

Of all Monte's choral books executed from 1514 onwards and all severely damaged during the flood, the Antiphonary D.8 is a significant and precious example. It is open (1988) at f. 146 R., where the initial L («Locutus est Dominus ad Habraam») figures a kneeling Abraham listening to the divine words, assisted by three angels; to the sides, related episodes. In the background the farewell embrace of Abraham under the portico of a large gothic building, while servants saddle a donkey. Above right, the sacrifice of Isaac.

The codex includes five other figurative miniatures. The most elaborate is found at f. 2, where the initial I includes the first stories from Genesis (*The Creation of Adam, the Creation of Eve, The Original Sin and the Expulsion of Adam and Eve from the Garden of Eden*); these evolve around the Tree of Sin (a fig instead of the more frequently depicted apple) which divides the rounded form of the letter into two parts.

The codex also includes, at f. 1 r (initial D: half figure of the Eternal Father); at f. 64 r. (initial N: half figure of a man); at f. 75 r. (initial D: bust of the Redeemer) and at f. 112 (initial D: Noah's ark).

The other three codices were decorated during the second decade of the sixteenth century by Frate Eustachio, a converted Dominican from the Convent of San Marco. They are, therefore, later (as are many of his other works for the Cathedral) than the famous Book of Psalms of 1505, which he decorated for his monastery and is still kept there.

The stylistic individuality of Frate Eustachio, one of the last followers of Monte di Giovanni, can be seen in the illustrations contained within the large capital letters. The pleasant and softly coloured scenes with their atmosphere of idyllic serenity remind us of the withdrawn monastic life of this Dominican miniature artist. His style has, in fact, been defined as the «Renaissance of the Monastery» (Francini Ciaranfi): the echoes of the Renaissance, already fully developed in contemporary painting, only just affected him. His figurative culture remains that of the fifteenth century and in particular, of Fra Angelico. The elegant and refined decorative elements — candelabra, gems and floral motifs with the stelae developed in volutes — are, however, in keeping with the times and reveal Frate Eustachio's qualities as a fine decorator and colourist.

The *Celebrative Gradual* marked *F. 6.32* contains a single figurative miniature: its attribution to Frate Eustachio is not definite. It is to be found at f. 45 v. inside the initial D («De ventre matris mee vocavit me») and represents the Baptism of Christ by St. John the Baptist. Further down, in the centre of the page, there is the coat of-arms of the Merchant's Guild (an eagle with a bound bale), the patrons of this work.

The *Antiphonary* marked *M. 25* is the only one of the three to be dated: the year MDXXVI (1526) is inscribed on the frontispiece of the codex (f. 1 r) and repeated on the inside of the frieze decorating the large miniature at f. 4 r. At present (1988), the Antiphonary is open at f. 70 r. with the scene of the Annunciation against an arched architectural background, painted inside the initial M («Missus est Gabriel»); above this, a tondo with God the Father in the act of benediction and the symbols of eternity.

Other illuminated initials can be found at f. 1 r. (the letter M: an angel indicates to an inscription above «EGO SCRIPSI», signifying the inspired origins of the sacred text), at f. 4 r. (very elaborate illumination on three sides with the coat-of-arms of the Opera del Duomo repeated three times and a slaughtered lamb, the symbol of sacrifice; in the letter D, the martyrdom of Sant'Agata); at f. 130 v. (initial C: San Zanobi, Bishop of Florence, enthroned between two angels).

The *Antiphonary* marked *E. 24* is at present (1988) open at f. 93 r. in which the initial V («Videntes

*Santa Maria del Fiore in circa 1864.*

Joseph a longe loquebantur fratres dicentes: Ecce sompniator venit ...») depicts the sons of Jacop grouped around a well, complaining about their brother Joseph, who approaches from afar. Once again the sacrificed lamb is featured in a tondo above the letter.

The other illuminated initials are at f. 1 r. (letter T: San Simone with a coronet, turban and saw); at f. 2 v., bordered by a decoration running along the external and the two minor margins with a sacrificed lamb below and the figures of Fortitude and Justice within small tondi; in the capital letter (letter E), St. Paul preaches holding a raised sword, against a hilly landscape with architecture. At f. 50 r. the letter T frames the scene of Isaac taking leave of Esau before the hunt, while his mother listens at the door.

The scene takes place within a porticoed courtyard and on a balcony above, Rebecca and Jacob prepare the deception with the sheepskin.

In order for the canons to be able to read these enormous choral books during the liturgical functions, they were placed on lecterns, called *badaloni*, in the middle of the Choir. In the centre of this room, there are two beautiful examples: the late eighteenth century Florentine lectern, in front of the display case containing the choral books, originates from the Cathedral whereas the sixteenth century Florentine example, bearing the Medici arms and decorated with fantastic figures and semi-precious stones within ovals, was almost certainly donated to the Baptistry by the Medici in occasion of a Prince's baptism (Settesoldi).

## The Cathedral's Treasures

The case along the entrance wall displays the following (from left to right): placed against the back wall, a *liturgical basin* in embossed copper and partly gilded with fine decorative motifs — vegetation, animals, winged musician putti, flowers, shells and butterflies — framing a central medallion representing the Madonna enthroned with Child (probably Santa Maria del Fiore) and two adoring angels. This is Florentine and dates from the first decade of the fifteenth century. The *chalice* is in embossed copper, dating to the end of

*Frate Eustachio, initial with the Annunciation, Antiphonary M. 25.*

*Monte di Giovanni, initial with Abraham and three angels, Antiphonary D.8.f. 146 r.*

38

the sixteenth or beginning of the seventeenth centuries and has a wide basin decorated with masks and volutes around a central rose.

Next to this, a *crozier* in gilded bronze with translucent enamel work, originating from Santa Maria del Fiore. Within the curl decorated with fretwork, there are the figures of the Madonna and Child blessing a kneeling Bishop. The enamel work on the hexagonal stem is in two segments and figures the Madonna, angels with the family crest of the Corsini family, the patron saints of Florence (Reparata, Stefano, Caterina d'Alessandria and John the Baptist) and the Saints Pietro and Lorenzo, who were of particular devotional importance to the Corsini. The crozier perhaps belonged to the Archbishop Amerigo Corsini, who held the position of Bishop in the Florentine diocese from 1411 to his death in about 1430.

The *chalice of Giulio de' Medici* is in embossed and chiselled copper and gilded silver. Within the three medallions decorated with inlay on the polylobed base are figured the *bust of the Madonna with Child*, the *Pietà* and a Medici crest surmounted by a cardinal's hat, perhaps the insignia of Giulio de' Medici, Archbishop of Florence from 1513 to 1523, and then Pope with the title of Clemente VII. The knot in the stem with embossed foliage, bears the inscription «HOC FACITE IN MEAM COMMEMORATIONEM». The chalice can be dated to the first half of the sixteenth century.

Following this, the *reliquary of San Simone Stilita*, originating from the Baptistry. This reliquary is particular in its formation: it is composed of two reliquaries of differing dates. The lower part in the form of a small hexagonal urn with crystal sides bearing the date 1398 contains, according to the inscription in gothic characters, certain relics which due to their age, are believed to have been donated by Carlo Magno, the mythical constructor of Florence. The upper part of the reliquary is fifteenth century and finely embossed, consisting of a hexagonal base (with the eagle with the bound bale, crest of the Merchant's Guild), a high, segmented stem and a cylindrical, crystal shrine containing other relics (perhaps added at the beginning of the seventeenth century by Bernardo Holzman: Ciardi Dupré). In the centre of the display case, there is a *chasuble (Farnese)*, belonging to the Accademia dell'Art del Disegno, but already transferred at the end of the nineteenth century to the new Museum of the Opera del Duomo, together with a frontal, which is still conserved in the Museum (not on display). The chasuble, of excellent technical crafts-

*Chasuble with the Farnese coat-of-arms.*

40

manship and high pictorial quality, consists of a satin mount (purple and brown), which is sumptuously decorated (*gros de Tours* appliqué embroidery; silver openwork; silver and silk painting).

The central framed column bears, within three pointed arches, three lilies above a ribbon, inscribed with the motto of the Farnese (ΘΕΟΘΕΝ ΑΥ Ε ΑΝΟΜΑΙ: "Divinitus auresco") at the centre a rampant half-unicorn, three hyacinths and a ribbon bearing the same Greek inscription. Below, the Farnese crest: a shield with a gold background and six blue lilies of France, surmounted by an archbishop's hat with twelve tassels in gold and silk (the crest and the motto of the Farnese can also be found on the frontal).

In the absence of documented data, these altar hangings had been related to the patronage of Alessandro Farnese and dated to the end of the first half, or beginning of the second half of the sixteenth century; stylistic analysis (Peri) had also led to a precise attribution to Pierin del Vaga for the frontal and Francesco Salviati for the chasuble. No explanation, however, was forthcoming as to their belonging to the Accademia del Disegno.

The history of these hangings has only recently been reconstructed (Zangheri). Cardinal Odoardo Farnese (1573-1626) commissioned them for the cell of Santa Maria Maddalena, founded by him in 1597 in the Convento di Camaldoli. He entrusted their design to the artist working for him in Rome at the same time, Annibale Carracci, who also realized the altar-piece with *Christ in Glory between Saints* (at present in the Galleria di Palazzo Pitti) for the same cell. Although these correspond in style to this artist's work, the drawings for the Farnese chasuble have proved to be the only known works of this type in the artist's production.

Following the Napoleonic suppression of the Monasteries, the hangings and frontal were transferred directly to the sacristy of the Chapel of the Accademia di San Luca.

On the right hand side of the display case, the *astylar cross* (processional) in gilded copper and decorated with tiny gilded stars on a blue enamelled background with gothic profiling and lobes. The figures decorating the cross — the crucifix and four evangelists at the terminal lobes (the pelican and the sun corresponding to the head and feet of Christ were a later addition) and, on the back of the three upper lobes, St. John the Baptist (above) and two prophets — reveal «the hand of an artist with a strong sense of the plastic, who knew how to instil a breath of classicism into the liveliest of Gothic traditions» (Becherucci). An artist who, in many ways, shows an affinity to the great sculptor and goldsmith, Luca della Robbia. One of the most singular pieces of goldsmith's work in the Museum is the *reliquary casket* in silver, partially gilded and covered with semi-precious stones of varying colours, probably originating from the Baptistry. This Florentine work of art dating from the end of the fifteenth century reproduces in a stylized miniature version the Medici tomb by Verrocchio in San Lorenzo and it is a perfect example of the diffused contemporary concept of the unity of the arts. The other *reliquary casket* is Venetian from the first half of the fifteenth century (?). It is in enamelled and gilded silver with tiny windows of rock crystal. The exterior is decorated with fantasic white animals, gold stars and moons on a deep blue background, the interior with gold stars against a green ground.

## 9. The Chapel

The display of the Cathedral Treasures continues in the small, octagonal chapel, which was built in 1954 expressly to house the important collection of reliquaries, from the Cathedral and Baptistry.

Apart from their purpose of holding and conserving the holy relics and indeed exalting their precious contents with their own magnificent appearance, the reliquaries were fitting objects to be admired and venerated by the faithful during solemn celebrative and religious festivals. For centuries, from the second half of the fifteenth century onwards, many of these, which belonged to San Giovanni were placed next to the religious hangings and other precious objects on the silver altar of the Baptistry (on display in the Museum) at the annual religious festivals of San Giovanni and the Perdono (13th January; the Baptism of Christ). These were occasions not only for a magnificent display of religious devotion but also for a public demonstration of the power and wealth of the Merchant's Guild, the patrons of the Baptistry. Examples of these include the reliquary of San Simone Stilita, the reliquaries of the arm of San Filippo Apostolo and the finger of the Baptist, the splendid reliquary of the «Libretto» and the reliquary of Anichino Corsi (displayed here).

After five or six centuries of use, nearly all the reliquaries in this chapel have undergone restoration and alteration, leading, in some cases, to the arbitrary recomposition of their various parts. Of particular note was the substantial restoration of all the Cathedral treasures undertaken at the beginning of the eighteenth century by the silversmith, Bernardo Holzman. These reliquaries have retained their artistic quality, which is often extremely high, and bear witness to three centuries of craftsmanship by Florentine goldsmiths. They are also of extraordinary importance both for the intrinsic value of the materials utilized and for their significance in the history of devotion.

In the first display case on the left wall, near to the entrance, the *reliquary of the index finger of St. John the Baptist* contains the holy relic of St. John the Baptist, considered the most important of his remains preserved in Florence. It was donated to the Florentine Republic by Baldassarre Coscia in a testamentary legacy. Antipope with the name of Giovanni XXIII, he was deposed by the Concilio di Costanza and came to Florence in 1419, where he died the following year. The reliquary in question was executed in 1698 at the expense of Francesco Maria Sergrifi, as the inscription on the front of the

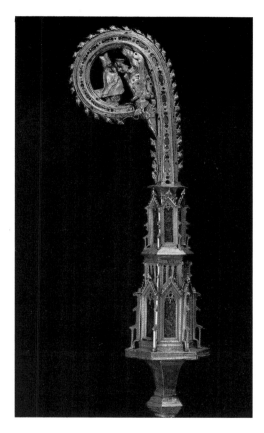

base testifies. The holy relic can be seen through oval apertures framed with precious stones and a triangular niche resting on a short, wide, knotted stem, which ends in a triangular base with curving facades. The crowning statue represents the Agnus Dei with the Cross.

The *reliquary of the Veil of Sant'Agata* (and other holy relics) in silver, bronze and gilded copper, is a masterpiece of Florentine baroque goldsmith's art; the twenty four groups of holy relics are divided by a rich and inspired decorative fantasy and each marked with a cartouche: in the central part of the reliquary in the base (containing the «velum S. Agathae») and at the top where a crown of leaves and a shell form the background for the urn, containing the ashes of the Baptist. All of these holy relics were given to Santa Maria del Fiore by the abbot of San Benedetto, don Federico Chiaramonte, in 1439, and were united in the present

Luca della Robbia and workshop, processional cross
(recto).

Florentine, second half of 15th century,
reliquary casket.

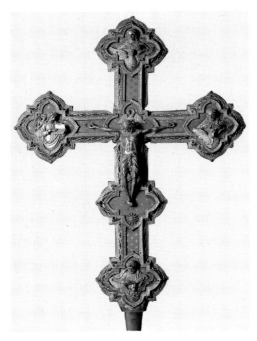

reliquary in 1714 by the request of Cosimo III de'
Medici.

The important legacy of the Benedectine abbot also
included the holy relic preserved in the above
*reliquary of the Chains of St. Peter* (gilded copper
and embossed silver), which is perhaps its original
container. It is finely decorated in the form of an
ark with four little angels on the lid and is gothic
both in design and execution.

In the following small display case, a series of
reliquaries originating from the Baptistry. The *reliquary of a finger bone of St. John the Baptist*, in
embossed and chiselled silver surmounted by a
statuette of the Baptist, could also have been
executed in parts with differing dates: the foot and
the frame date from the end of the fifteenth or
beginning of the sixteenth centuries whereas the
upper part including the cylindrical shrine, although greatly altered in the eighteenth century,
date from the fourteenth century together with the
oldest parts of the reliquary (Ciardi Dupré). According to the seventeenth and eighteenth century
tradition, the reliquary of the Baptist came from
Constantinople and reached Florence in 1392.

The following *reliquary of the Jaw of St. John the
Evangelist* perhaps contains the holy relic also
originating from Constantinople, donated by the
Venetian noblewoman, Madonna Grioni (wife of
the Florentine, Pietro Torrigiani, who was the
«cameriere» to Giovanni Cantacuzeno, the Emperor of Constantinople) to the Baptistry of St. John.
The reliquary is in embossed silver and gilded
copper with cast parts and was realized in 1564 by
Pietro Cerluzi, goldsmith to the grand-ducal Office
of Works at the time of Cosimo I de' Medici.

The hexagonal base is in the shape of a pyramid's
trunk, the segmented stem opens into a wide cup,
on which rests the arched aedicola with the holy
relic; surmounting this, the statue of St. John the
Baptist, surrounded by six putti seated on the frame
of the aedicola.

The *reliquary of the Arm of San Filippo* is, in actual
fact, to be considered in two distinct parts. The first
part, the hexagonal urn with rectangular panels in
rock crystal, bears the inscription stating the origin
of the reliquary containing relics of many saints
(including Stefano and Pantaleone) from Constantinople in 1394, and their collocation in this urn in
1398. The second part is the actual reliquary of the
Arm of San Filippo; a most precious holy relic
donated to the Basilica of San Giovanni in 1204. It
is enclosed in a glass tube, which in turn is inserted
into a small temple with high pilasters and buttress-

es, decorated with small statues of the prophets. This is crowned by a cupola of crystal with six vaulted ribs decorated with rampant dragons, upon which rests the small gilded silver statue of San Filippo.

The latter has been attributed to the goldsmith Andrea del Vagliente, active in Florence in the first half of the fifteenth century.

Higher up, the *ex-voto of Anichino Corsi*, executed in 1447, is the only remaining example of the work of the goldsmith, Rinaldo di Giovanni di Ghino. The great branch of coral, with a simple, partly gilded silver mount, was donated to the Baptistry by Anichino Corsi (of whom there is no documented information), who had acquired it as booty, subsequent to an expedition against the Moors (as the inscription on the knot of the framework states: «ex spoliis maurorum hoc coralium huic templo dicavit Anichinus Corsis»). Coral, full of magical and symbolic significance, had from antiquity onwards been considered to have the power to keep away danger and evil spirits.

The third display case contains a single piece, the great *Reliquary Cross of the Passion*. One of the most precious pieces in the collection, it is in gold, polychrome enamel and precious stones. The Grand-duchess Maria Maddalena d'Austria, wife of Cosimo II, donated it to the Cathedral to house the ancient and valued relics of the Passion (above) and a splinter from the Sacred Cross (inside a central crown of thorns). The exquisite workmanship has been attributed to Odoardo Vallet (Becherucci), but it is actually the documented work of the court goldsmith, Cosimo Merlini, and had already been completed in 1618 (Fock), even though the pedestal bears the date of 1620. The base for the cross in gilded bronze, bearing the date 1700, was added by Bernardo Holzman.

Proceeding past the altar, in the first display case on the opposite wall; the *reliquary of the Santi Apostoli*, originating from the Cathedral, is a fine example of sophisticated Florentine goldsmith's work dating to the middle of the fifteenth century.

It is in embossed, gilded copper. The monstrance, in the form of a hexagonal temple with columns and a small cupola surmounted with a cross, contains the holy relics (of the Saints Pietro, Paolo, Andrea, Iacopo, of San Brizio Vescovo and Beato Ippolito Galantini) and is sustained by a stem, delicately worked in segments with fretwork and embossing (the name of the patron appears in the central knot «NICHOLO BARTOLINI»), which expands into the base with eight circular lobes.

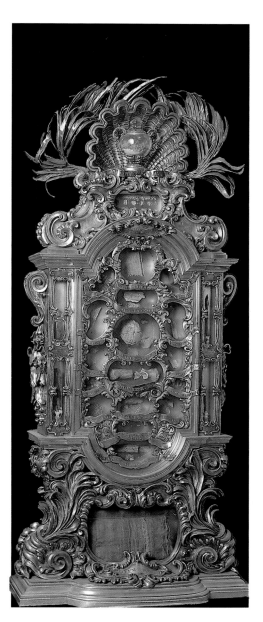

43

44

Perhaps the most important of all the reliquaries of the Museum is that of *the «Libretto»* in the centre of the display case.

The shrine, completed in 1501 by the Florentine goldsmith, Giovanni di Paolo Sogliani, is in partially gilded silver and decorated with enamels. It is composed of one large polylobed base (decorated with two tondi in enamel figuring the eagle with the bound bale of the Merchants' Guild), a corbel with four volutes and an elegant little temple crowned with a statue of the Baptist. This was expressly made to contain the actual reliquary, visible through the crystal windows, called the «Libretto», a work from the second half of the fourteenth century by a French goldsmith.

The «Libretto» is a polyptych in gold with enamel and precious stones, composed of various folding compartments. The upper part of the central compartment bears an illustrated miniature (recto: *Crucifix* with the *Madonna, San Giovanni Evangelista* and the *Magdalene;* verso: the *Trinity, Carlo V* King of France with his wife, *Giovanna di Borbone*), whereas the fronts of the compartments have little spaces inside three-mullioned windows containing various holy relics; the central one holds the most important examples (the instruments of the Passion).

On the back there is an inscription in French stating that Carlo V of France (1364-'80) donated the reliquary to his brother Luigi, the Duke d'Angiò. Subsequently, the reliquary was documented in the collection of Piero de' Medici, il «Gottoso» (1416-'69). Following the expulsion of the Medici from Florence, it was acquired for the Baptistry in the last decade of the fifteenth century by the Merchants' Guild, who commissioned Sogliani to provide the shrine.

The *reliquary of Santa Reparata*, originating from the Cathedral, is signed by the Florentine artist Francesco Vanni (underneath the knot: "FRANCISCUS NANNI (sic) DE FLORENTIA ME FECIT"), who was active in the second half of the sixteenth century.

Notwithstanding alterations made in the seventeenth century with the addition of the shrine containing the reliquary, (fragments of a rib of Santa Reparata), it is still possible to admire the elegance of the stem with polylobed base and small crowning tabernacle with mullioned windows.

The following display case holds the *reliquary of the Arm of San Giusto*, originating from the Cathedral, of French manufacture and dating from the eighteenth century. It is in silver, partially gilded and decorated with precious stones. It takes the form of an arm in the act of benediction clothed with a double sleeve (the internal sleeve bears a gothic inscription, which translated reads as follows: «Herewith you find the arm of Beato Giusto, Archbishop of Lyons, placed here by Bernarduccio, son of Lese the Soldier»). The reliquary can be seen through an oval aperture.

The *reliquary of San Gerolamo* is of Florentine craftsmanship dating to the second half of the fifteenth century (Antonio di Salvi?) in silver, partially gilded, embossed and decorated with translucent enamels. Above the high polylobed base, two arms branch out, supporting two angels, which flank a hexagonal aedicola in the form of a small temple with arches containing the jaw of San Gerolamo. This is surmounted by two superimposed cylindrical niches with pilasters and columns, which contain the relic of the bone from the arm of the Saint. The enamel work (partly missing the glass layer) on the base and on the temple depicts the cycle of stories relating to the life of San Gerolamo. Various inscriptions (on the upper part, below the lid, on the architrave of the central temple, on the knot of the base and on the book of the angel) specify the contents of the reliquary (the jaw and bone from the arm of San Gerolamo) and also state that this formed part of a group of holy relics donated to the Cathedral by the abbot Federico di Chiaromonte in 1439, later placed in the present reliquary commissioned by the Canon Jacopo Mannelli in 1487.

The *reliquary of San Filippo Neri*, realized in the seventeenth century, perhaps in the granducal workshops, also comes from the Cathedral. It is in the form of an oval monstrance in embossed and cast silver with a traditional gothic lobed base; it is surmounted by a medallion with the symbols of the Passion within minutely detailed fretwork.

In the final display case, the *reliquary of Sant'Antonio Abate*, donated by the Captains of the Guelph Party to Santa Maria del Fiore in 1514, was executed by Antonio di Salvi Salvucci and is in silver and gilded copper with translucent enamel work.

It is in the form of a hexagonal temple with a crowning cupola, surmounted by a small statue of Sant'Antonio Abate (to whose protection was attributed the success of the Guelphs and their return to Florence, following the fall of the Ciompi in 1382). An anonymous artist was responsible for the refined designs of the enamelling (very damaged), the base (note the lamb with the standard: the crest of the Wool Guild, patron of Santa Maria del Fiore, and the eagle with dragon, that of the Guelphs) and of the temple, with the representation of the patron saints of Florence (*Giovanni, Barnaba, Vittore Papa*) and of *S. Ludovico*, King of France, Protector of the Guelphs.

Finally, the *reliquary of the two phalanges of the finger of St. John the Baptist* from Santa Maria del Fiore in partially gilded silver and decorated with translucent enamel. This has suffered much alteration following sixteenth and seventeenth century restoration, particularly the aedicola which encloses the rock crystal vase with the holy relic itself (the history of the relic, which came from Constantinople, is contained in the long, partly fragmented inscription engraved on the reliquary). The original parts, clearly Gothic (dating to the first decade of

the fifteenth century), can still be admired. These are perhaps the work of Ghiberti's workshop and include the polylobed base with steps bordered with fine fretwork, the tall, slender stem in two segments and the spire. The stem and the support in the form of an upturned pyramid on which the aedicola rests, are decorated with enamel work — floral motifs, *Madonna with Child, Angels* and *Saints* — in which, although very damaged, Becherucci has noted a refined version of the international Gothic.

To the side of the marble altar (1954), there is a marble *spiral column*, decorated with cosmatesque mosaic (gilded and polychrome glass). This is one of the few surviving from the Arnolfi facade for Santa Maria del Fiore and has since been adapted for use as a candelabra with the addition of a nineteenth century base and socket.

The altar-piece with the *Madonna between S. Caterina and S. Zanobi* (tempera on panel; dated on the step between the names of the two saints: «Anno D(omi)ni MCCCXXXIIII die XXV februarii», 1335, modern calendar) is attributed to Bernardo Daddi, one of the most prolific of the first generation artists to be influenced by Giotto and responsible for the almost contemporary Tabernacolo del Bigallo. The Virgin is three-quarter length within a frame, in her hand a book inscribed with the prayer of two donors (lower down): "Sweet Virgin, Mary of Bagnuolo begs you to pray to Him, whose protection will grant me grace for that which I need".

## 10. The Entrance Hall

Leaving the chapel and crossing the Room of the Choral Books and that of the Cathedral Facade, we return to the Entrance Hall, which contains sculptural and architectural fragments resulting from the restoration of the Cathedral, Baptistry and Bell Tower.

There are numerous *plaques* on the walls with sepulchral inscriptions dating to various periods and bearing the coats-of-arms of noted Florentine families (Pilli, Tornaquinci, Falconieri, Chellini, Portinari, Guidotti, Bargiacchi, De Rinaldi, Citadini, Pecori, Banchini, Busini, Benricevuti, Sostegni). These originate from the cemetery of the former Cathedral of S. Reparata, located in front of the facade and along its south side. They were removed partly during the construction of the new Cathedral, Santa Maria del Fiore, which came to occupy a portion of the land formerly used for the cemetery, and partly during the realization of the present facade in 1887.

*Paolo di Giovanni Sogliani, reliquary of the*
*«Libretto» (1501).*

*Cosimo Merlini, the cross of Maria Maddalena
d'Austria with the holy relics of the Passion
(1618, with 18th century base).*

*Attributed to Antonio di Salvi, reliquary of San Gerolamo (1487).*

The hall also contains the *remains of the old baptismal font and choir enclosure of the Baptistry*, destroyed in 1576 by Bernardo Buontalenti (who later favoured the demolition of the Arnolfian facade) on occasion of its celebrative decoration for the baptism of Prince Filippo, son of the Granduke Francesco I de' Medici. These are panels or fragments of panels fortunately recovered at different times and from different places after they had been reutilized as salvage material following the destruction.

Some are rectangular, decorated with intaglio in a geometrical lattice with rosettes against a background of inlaid black marble, either on one side or on both (two examples can be seen on special revolving mounts under the window).

Others are square with a central tondo or rhombus, each framing a rosette against a background of geometrically inlaid black and white marble. The particular characteristics of the Florentine Romanesque (geometric interwoven patterns and the use of two colours), which were later to be used in the

Baptistry and San Miniato, are already noticeable here.

Dante mentions that these panels partly derive from the baptismal font in the «bel San Giovanni» (*Inferno*, canto XIX and *Paradiso*, canto XXV). Although it is now certain that it was situated in the centre of the Baptistry, there is some doubt concerning its typology. It was probably square, with four small drains at each corner (a square stone base with a groove for water has been found), inside an octagonal wall which joined it to the choir, also square in form.

There is controversy surrounding the date of the font (and therefore also of the panels): it oscillates between 1128 (date of the first documented baptism in San Giovanni) and the first quarter of the thirteenth century, the date of the money-box and actual marble pavement.

On the wall facing the window, there is a group of decorative *fragments from the Porta «della Mandorla»*, on the north side of Santa Maria del Fiore (facing via dei Servi); the last of the Cathedral doors to be realised (late fourteenth century and the first decades of the fifteenth century), and the most important. The ornate decoration of this door included a frieze, which ran the entire length of the broken arch with busts of angels alternating with foliage and mythological figures. The two pieces belong to the latter group, one with *an angel within a hexagon and a figure of Hercules inside an acanthus bush*, the other with a *half figure of an angel with in part of a hexagon and a small putto between acanthus leaves*. These are attributed to the workshop of Niccolò di Piero Lamberti and represent some of the first sporadic but significant signs at the end of the forteenth century of the future classical style.

The *Christ in pietà*, with arms that distend beyond the pentagon which frames it, was situated at the apex of the same broken arch.

Although formerly attributed to Nanni di Bartolo, called il Rosso, more recently Donatello has been considered its author (Bellosi).

Above this group of fragments a *lunette* in glazed earthenware with *San Zanobi between two angels*. The work, with its white figures against a blue background, is attributed to the workshop of Andrea della Robbia (1435-1528).

The right hand of the Saint has been restored and the head re-attached. Originally, this lunette decorated the door of the Compagnia di San Zanobi, which had its offices in the Rectory of Santa Maria del Fiore.

*Attributed to Bernardo Daddi, Madonna*
*between Santa Caterina and San Zanobi.*

*Panel of the original baptismal font of the Baptistry.*

*The mezzanine with the Pietà by Michelangelo.*

### The Mezzanine

The mezzanine is at the top of the first flight of stairs. It is a rather narrow location for the most famous piece in the Opera collection: the *Pietà* by Michelangelo, the so-called *Pietà* del Duomo or the *Pietà* Bandini. It seems opportune to introduce the visitor to the celebrated *Pietà*, using the two principle sources of information concerning the life and works of Michelangelo; the artistic biographies of his contemporaries, Giorgio Vasari and Ascanio Condivi.

52

«Now he has in hand a work in marble which he is doing for his own pleasure; being a man who is full of ideas and energy, he naturally produces something every day. This is a group of four figures over life-size, consisting of a Christ deposed from the cross, whose dead body is sustained by His mother, as she slips her breast, arms, and knee under His body in a remarkable pose. However, she is assisted from above by Nicodemus, who, erect and firm on his legs, with a display of vigorous strength supports the body under the arms; and from the left side she is assisted by one of the Marys, who, although visibly deeply grieved, nevertheless does not fail in the task to which the mother, in her extreme sorrow, is not equal. The released Christ falls with all His limbs slackened, but in a very different position from the one Michelangelo did for the marchioness of Pescara or the one of the Madonna della Febbre. It would be impossible to describe the beauty and the emotions shown in the grieving and sorrowful faces of the anguished mother and all the others; therefore let this suffice. I really mean to say that it is something rare and one of the more exacting works that he has done to date, chiefly because all the figures are perceived distinctly and the draperies of any one figure are not to be confused with those of the other».

A. Condivi, *The life of Michelangelo*, Roma 1553, translation by Alice Sedgwick Wohl, Oxford, 1976.

"The spirit and genius of Michelangelo could not remain idle; and so, since he was unable to paint, he set to work on a piece of marble, intending to carve four figures in the round and larger than life-size (including a dead Christ) to amuse and occupy himself and also, as he used to say himself, because using the hammer kept his body healthy. This Christ, taken down from the cross, is supported by Our Lady, by Nicodemus (planted firmly on his feet as he bends down and assists her) and by one of the Marys who also gives her help on perceiving the failing strength of his mother, whose grief makes the burden intolerable. Nowhere else can one see a dead form to compare with this figure of Christ; he is shown sinking down with his limbs hanging limp and he lies in an attitude altogether different not only from that of any other of Michelangelo's figures but from that of any other figures ever made. This work, the fruit of intense labour, was a rare achievement in a single stone and truly inspired; but, as will be told later on, it remained unfinished and suffered many misfortunes, although Michelangelo had intended it to go at the foot of the altar where he hoped to place his own tomb. Michelangelo used to work every day, for recreation, on the block of stone with four figures that we have already mentioned; and at this time he broke it into pieces. He did this either because it was hard and full of emery and the chisel often struck sparks from it, or perhaps because his judgement was so severe that he was never content with anything he did.

Anyhow, he gave the broken Pietà to Francesco Bandini. At that time on the introduction of Francesco Bandini and Donato Giannotti, the Florentine sculptor, Tiberio Calcagni, struck up a close friendship with Michelangelo. And then one day when he was at his house, after they had discussed things together for a long time, Tiberio asked Michelangelo why he had broken the Pietà (which was in the house) and had wasted all his marvellous efforts. Michelangelo answered that the reason for this was the importunity of his servant Urbino who had nagged him every day to finish it; and as well as this a piece had broken off from the arm of the Madonna. And these things, he said, as well as other mishaps including his finding a crack in the marble, had made him so hate the work that he had lost patience and broken it; and he would have smashed it completely had not his servant Antonio persuaded him to give it to someone just as it was.

After he heard this, Tiberio spoke to Bandini, who was anxious to have something by Michelangelo, and Bandini then persuaded him to promise two hundred gold crowns to Antonio, if he would beg Michelangelo to allow Tiberio, using Michelangelo's models, to finish the statue for Bandini.

This would mean that Michelangelo's labours would not have been thrown away, he said. Michelangelo was happy with this arrangement, and he gave the block to them as a gift. It was immediately carried off and subsequently put together by Tiberoi who added God knows how many new pieces. All the same, it still stayed unfinished because of the death of Bandini, of Michelangelo, and of Tiberio.

G. Vasari, *The Lives of the Artists*, Florence 1550 and 1568, a selection translated by George Bull, 1965

"Once Vasari was sent by Julius III at the first hour of the night to Michelangelo's house to fetch a design, and he found Michelangelo working on the marble Pietà that he subsequently broke. Recognizing who it was by the knock, Michelangelo left his work and met him with a lamp in his hand.

After Vasari had explained what he was after, he sent Urbino upstairs for the drawing and they started to discuss other things. Then Vasari's eyes fell on the leg of the Christ on which Michelangelo was working and making some alterations, and he started to look closer. But to stop Vasari seeing it, Michelangelo let the lamp fall from his hand, and they were left in darkness. Then he called Urbino to fetch a light, and meanwhile coming out from the enclosure where he had been working he said:
«I am so old that death often tugs my cloak for me to go with him. One day my body will fall just like that lamp, and my light will be put out".

G. Vasari, *The Lives of the Artists*, Florence 1550 and 1568, a selection translated by George Bull, 1965

*The Pietà by Michelangelo.*

*The Pietà by Michelangelo, detail.*

The majority of critics date the realization of the *Pietà* between the end of the 1540's, perhaps following the death of Vittoria Colonna (1547), with whom Michelangelo had a profound friendship, and 1555, when the idea was definitively abandoned following an attempt to destroy the unfinished statue. The *Pietà*, which Michelangelo had originally considered for his own tomb, was acquired in 1561 by Francesco Bandini, the Florentine sculptor and architect, who entrusted its restoration to Michelangelo's pupil, Tiberio Calcagni (this consisted in the reparation of the breakages and the completion of the unfinished parts, based on the artist's own designs).

The statue remained in the Roman gardens of Bandini, at Montecavallo, even though Vasari attempted to have it transferred to Florence for the tomb of Michelangelo in Santa Croce. It is not clear the exact circumstances of its arrival in Florence in the second half of the seventeenth century (1674?), following interest shown by the Granduke Cosimo III de' Medici. Originally situated in the crypt of San Lorenzo, the *Pietà* was transferred to Santa Maria del Fiore in 1722, again following the wishes of Cosimo. It was positioned behind the main altar, taking the place of a statue of Adam and Eve by Baccio Bandinelli. It was then moved to the first chapel of the north transept, and remained in Santa Maria del Fiore until March 1980, when it was displayed in Santo Stefano al Ponte in occasion of the Medici exhibition.

Subsequently it was not returned to the Cathedral and in April 1981, following a much disputed decision, it was placed in the Museum of the Opera del Duomo.

Michelangelo repeatedly returned to the theme of the «Pietà» in old age with a series of drawings and three tormented sculptures - very far from the tranquility of his youthful period in Rome - none of which were to be completed. They do not actually correspond to the traditional concept of the «pietà» (a representation of the dead Christ supported by Angels and Saints, a pictorial theme which can be traced back to the thirteenth century), but fuse elements of this with similar motifs from the Deposition from the Cross and the Entombment of Christ. The Florentine *pietà* is characterised by the three figures surrounding Christ, united in the all-enveloping rhythm of a common action; that of sustaining the body and supporting and consoling each other. The central motif of the composition remains that of the lifeless body of Christ whose abandoned limbs sink in a slow and all-pervading motion

downwards — from the double counterposition of the torso and the leg to the heavy right arm twisted round from the shoulder on which the head reclines — against which those present can offer no resistance.

The Magdalene occupies the privileged position traditionally assigned to the Virgin, who is, instead, seated to the left, stretched out towards her son, her face mingling with his hair. A standing figure dominating the group has been identified as Nicodemus, the converted Pharisee recorded in the Book of St. John as present at the entombment of Christ (some have identified the figure as Joseph of Arimathea, the disciple who gave his own tomb for the body of Christ). In his features, according to Vasari, can be found a self-portrait of the aged Michelangelo and this identification gives an idea of the artist's personal involvement in this *Pietà* conceived for his own tomb.

The project was, however, abandoned before completion; according to Vasari, Michelangelo had already attempted to destroy the statue, breaking it in various places. He was either irritated by the faults in the marble, or by the requests of his servant, Urbino, or quite simply, dissatisfied with himself. One can, in fact, note cracks around the hand of the Virgin and on the left arm of Christ, whereas the left leg is completely missing (this is in contrast to all the sixteenth and seventeenth century reproductions, in which it appears with the foot resting on the ground).

It is certain that the statue remained unfinished and that Tiberio Calcagni made some measured additions. He was a pupil of Michelangelo and was responsible for the completion of the Magdalene and a series of minor retouches, which have not been definitely identified. Michelangelo was undoubtedly responsible for the most part of the right hand side of the group; the complete merges with the incomplete in a technique created by the artist himself (even if in this case an interruption in the artist's work must be assumed). The smooth surfaces of Christ's body thrown into relief by the light falling on the decomposed surfaces contrast with the irregular masses of the figures of Nicodemus and the Madonna and accentuate death's isolation, whereas the expressive concentration on the male faces is reflected in the vibrant luminosity of the stone surfaces, which bear the typical hatchmarks of the gradine. Although the face of the Madonna has only been sketched, its intensely expressive nature reveals a sentiment of profound grief.

In Michelangelo's development, this *Pietà* is linked

to two other works realized late in his life; the *Pietà* of Palestrina (Florence, Accademia, which is not universally attributed to Michelangelo) and the *Pietà* Rondanini (Milan, Museo del Castello Sforzesco), on which he worked almost up to his death. They reflect an increasing spiritualization of the plastic material; they «represent the stages of an increasingly intense meditation; they express a growing spiritualization of the form beyond all limits; they bear witness to a search for a new language in the disintegration of the plastic material, an extremely sensitive and passionate language, capable of perceiving the most hidden murmurs of the heart». (Carli).

## 12. The Stairs

Running along the wall of the stairwell, eight *corbels* (14th Century?), from an unidentified part of the Cathedral's exterior, support eight *heads* with differing dates and provenances; three in pietra serena and five in marble. Of particular note are the final two examples (in marble) on the right hand side ascending, the provenances and attributions to which are still the subject of critical debate.

The first, attributed to the Sienese sculptor, Tino di Camaino, is probably a fragment of a statue of St. John the Baptist, formerly situated over the south door of the Baptistry, where he was represented in the act of baptizing Christ, who was to be found in the centre. The other, also probably originating from the Baptistry's decoration, is a work of high quality and perhaps executed by Andrea Pisano.

At the top of the stairs, the door leading to the Room of the Choir Galleries is flanked by two large capitals in inlaid marble with bas-relief (Florentine, 15th Century), provenance unknown; on the walls above them, *two fresco fragments with the heads of the apostles* (Peter and Paul?), work of Bicci di Lorenzo. They were realized in 1440 as part of a cycle figuring the apostles to decorate the pilasters and the naves inside Santa Maria del Fiore.

They were detached in 1840 when there was a general redecoration of the interior of the Cathedral. Crossing the Room of the Choir Galleries, we reach that of the Bell Tower Panels.

## 13. The Room of the Bell Tower Panels

The panels of the Bell Tower of Santa Maria del Fiore have been arranged in this room in two sequences, one above the other, following their original disposition. They were transferred to the Museum in the years 1965-'67 for conservation reasons; they have been substituted by plaster casts *in situ*.

The Bell Tower was begun in 1334 on Giotto's design. At his death (1337) only the lowest sequence of hexagonal panels had been completed. His successor, Andrea Pisano (Master Builder from 1337 to 1347), added a similar sequence above, decorated with lozenge-shaped panels. He introduced a variation in the scheme in the above two sequences by dividing each order with two parastades and including a series of statue niches. The final three orders, perforated by two - and three - mullioned windows without sculptural decoration, are the work of Francesco Talenti, who completed the Bell Tower in 1459.

The vast iconographic programme of the plastic decoration (reliefs and statues) was to represent of the various stages in the process of salvation inherent in the story of man. These related to precise descriptions, elaborated by scholasticism and deeply-rooted in the conscience and imagination of mediaeval Europe; a unique programme for a Bell-Tower but frequently used on the facades of churches in the North of Italy.

The series of hexagonal panels, forming the first order, create a clear and organic cycle; that of the Creation and the progressive civilization of man through his various activities. There are the *Artes mechanicae* (including the figurative arts, for the manual skill involved) and other activities directed towards social organization, represented by their mythical inventors.

In the order above, within the lozenges, the *Planets* represent the elementary forces, together with the moral (*Virtù*) and the intellectual (*Artes Liberales*) forces, contributing to the elevation of human toil above pure necessity, and the preparation of man for God's salvation. Finally, the *Sacraments* are the instruments of Salvation. The cycle is concluded in the following room of the Museum with the third order: statues representing those figures from Antiquity and from the Old Testament, who had prophesied and prepared the way for the coming of Christ — Kings, Sybils, Prophets and Patriarchs.

Hypotheses about such an organically articulate programme (Trachtemberg, Moschowitz) concern its reflection of the political and social changes, which took place in Florence between the 1330's and 1340's. The fast expanding economy of the 1330's corresponded to the exaltation of the activity of man (first order), whereas the repeated crises ending in the plague of 1348 are reflected by the hope in God's intervention (the above orders).

The hexagonal panels, which had perhaps blue plaster backgrounds similar to the reliefs of the above order, are attributed to Andrea Pisano even though the initial panels (east side) with stories taken from Genesis were positioned at the same time as the marble covering and therefore, simultaneously with Giotto's direction of the works and Andrea Pisano's work on the first bronze door for the Baptistry. Giotto, whom various critics (Pucci, Ghiberti and Vasari) cite as the author of certain reliefs and models (the famous «provvedimenti» of Ghiberti), probably inspired the sense of reality and dramatic concentration of these scenes. The last five were executed by Luca della Robbia between 1437 and 1439 following the abolition of the gallery linking the Bell Tower to the Cathedral.

The sequence of the panels, restored to its original form in the Museum display, should be read from the first panel on the right on the wall facing the entrance, corresponding to the east side of the Tower, then to the left following the walls, which correspond to the south, east and north sides of the Tower.

The wall facing the entrance (west side): *the Creation of Man; the Creation of Eve, the First Work, Jabal, Jubal, Tubalcain, Noah* (the biblical in-

ventors of, respectively, stock-raising, music, metallurgy and the vintage).

The left wall (south side): *Gionitus,* inventor of astronomy, *Armatura* or *the Art of Building, Medicine, Hunting* (Equitation), *Lanificium* (the art of weaving), *Phroneus,* the inventor of legislation, *Daedalus,* ancestor of artists. Entrance wall (east side): *Navigation, Hercules and Cacus* (liberation of the world from monsters, or Social Justice), *Agriculture.* Right wall (north side): *Phidias* (sculpture), *Apelle* (painting). These are followed by the panels by Luca della Robbia.

It is difficult to evaluate the contribution of the various artists working on this cycle, which was realized on site at Santa Maria del Fiore with the typical mediaeval technique of production: the workshop («bottegha»). The «maestri», craftsmen and apprentices collaborated on the same projects and the provenance of each single piece was of secondary importance. Consequently, there are clear fluctuations in the qualitative level of each part of the cycle (*Gionitus, Armatura, Medicine* and *Phroneus* were probably the work of apprentices) but simultaneously, a coherent stylistic development. The first hexagon, figuring the stories taken from Genesis, are linked to the contemporary

*Andrea Pisano, the Creation of Adam.*

58

*Andrea Pisano, Stock-raising (Jabal).*

*Andrea Pisano, Metallurgy (Tubalcain).*

*Andrea Pisano, Navigation.*

*Andrea Pisano, Daedalus.*

*Andrea Pisano, Agriculture.*

*Andrea Pisano, Sculpture, detail.*

61

*Andrea Pisano, Architecture.*

*Luca della Robbia, Music with Orpheus.*

Gothic character of the Porta di San Giovanni, in which attention is concentrated on details, on the landscape and on the narrative development of the action. Although there is a classical study of the nude (the *Creation of Adam* and the *Creation of Eve*), in general these first reliefs appear the least Giottoesque, even though they were executed before Giotto's death.

An increasing accent on monumentality appears in the composition of the panels from *Tubalcain* on, and this is usually synthesized in the action which takes place around a single figure or theme. The plasticity of the volumes and the fundamental specification of the spaces permit an exceptionally concentrated means of expression, reflected in the emotive tension of the faces and attitudes.

Amongst the most significant examples, demonstrating the importance of Andrea's participation, are *Tubalcain, Daedalus, Navigation* and *Agriculture*. Giotto's teaching is fundamental here, in addition to precise references to the Antique (*Hercules and Cacus, Sculpture*) which already anticipate the Renaissance in the fifteenth century.

The five panels by Luca della Robbia represent the Liberal Arts, but no agreement has been reached concerning the interpretation of the single subjects: *Grammar*, with Priscian (or Donatus), *Logic and Dialectics* with Plato and Aristotle, *Music* with Orpheus, *Arithmetic and Geometry* with Euclid and Pythagoras, *Astrology* with Pythagoras (*Harmony* with Tubalcain hammering on an anvil and thus producing the first musical sounds).

The typical characteristics of Luca's style; composed, solemn rhythms and a serene use of the human figure (particularly evident in *Music* and *Astrology*) were influenced by a variety of tendencies, from Ghiberti to Jacopo della Quercia and Donatello (above all, in the more animated scenes, such as *Logic and Dialectics* and *Arithmetic and Geometry*).

On the same wall, a *Madonna with Child*, a relief against a background formed of blue majolica lozenges. It is within an original lunette and attributed to Andrea Pisano (circa 1342-'43). Its original position was over a door used by the Church personnel on the north side of the Bell Tower, connected to the Cathedral by means of a gallery (demolished in 1431). The private nature of its location is reflected in the intimate atmosphere of the composition; the Madonna stretches out her arms in an affectionate gesture (symbolic of the *Ecce Agnus Dei*) but is vivaciously pushed away by the Child.

*Luca della Robbia, Logic and Dialectics
with Plato and Aristotle.*

64

The lozenge-shaped panels, the grounds of which are encrusted with blue, are from the School of Andrea Pisano (there is some debate about the names of his pupils).

Proceeding, as with the panels already mentioned, along the wall facing the entrance. (west side): *Saturn* (with the wheel of time), *Jupiter* (in a Christian interpretation as a monk with a chalice and cross, symbols of the faith), *Mars* (an armed warrior), *The Sun or Apollo* (a crowned youth with sceptre and sun-disc), *Venus* (with two lovers), *Mercury* (as a teacher with two pupils), *the Moon* (with a fountain, indicating the lunar action on water).

Left wall (south side): *Faith* (with the cross and chalice), *Charity* (with a cornucopia and a heart), *Hope* (with arms raised towards a crown), *Prudence* (with two heads — one of Youth and one of Age — with a knotted serpent and a mirror), *Justice* (with the scales and sword), *Temperance* (in the act of pouring liquid from one vessel to another), *Strength* (clothed in the skin of an animal, with a club and shield).

Entrance wall (east side): *Astronomy* (with the terrestial globe), *Music* (with a lyre), *Geometry* (with the compasses and book), *Grammar* (with a sceptre in the act of teaching), *Rhetoric* (with shield and sword), *Logic* (with scissors), *Arithmetic* (in the act of counting).

Right wall (north side): *Baptism*, *Confession*, *Matrimony*, *Priesthood* (only the triangular top of the panel has survived, which was to be adapted to the lunette below), *Confirmation*, *the Eucharist* and *Extreme Unction*.

The style of these reliefs, developing from the formal language of Andrea Pisano, demonstrates a formal solidity, a plasticity of volume and an essentiality in the composition, which result in the particularly high quality of the series of the Planets. Amongst others, the author of the panels of the *Sacraments* (right wall) is to be distinguished. At one time they were considered the work of Alberto Arnoldi, but they are now attributed to Maso di Bianco, noted above all as a follower of Giotto and his pupil on the Santa Croce site where, in about 1340 he decorated the Cappella Bardi di Vernio with frescoes of the Stories of San Silvestro. The panels with the seven sacraments, represented by the ritual act of their conferment stylistically correspond to the work of Maso in the picturesque taste for narrative detail (above all, in the *Baptisim* and the *Extreme Unction*) and the tendency to simplify the masses, which stand out against the neutral

*Andrea Pisano, Madonna with Child.*

66

backgrounds. Above the entrance, there are three small statues, originally located on the pinnacles of the door on the east side of the Bell Tower (these have also been replaced *in loco* with plaster casts). They were placed there in 1431 but had been executed some decades before this.

The central figure of the *Redeemer* (?) is quite poor in quality; attributed to the school of Francesco Talenti (1360 circa), it is of little interest. The *two little prophets* on each side have been severely damaged due to their lengthy exposure outdoors, but even so, are works of quality with a particularly lively plasticity.

Previously attributed to Nanni di Bartolo, called «il Rosso», they have more recently been considered the work of the young Donatello, while still part of Ghiberti's workshop, and have been dated to about 1410 (Herzner).

### 14. The Room of the Choir Galleries

This is one of the earliest rooms in the Museum and dates to its foundation in 1891. The idea of the Museum arose from the need to reconstruct the two dismantled *choir galleries* («cantorie») by Donatello and Luca della Robbia, and to provide them with a suitable location. Between 1936 and 1946, the sixteen statues decorating the niches of the third order of the Bell Tower were also transferred here (substituted *in situ* by plaster casts). Recently (1972) the wooden statue of the *Magdalene* by Donatello from the Baptistry has also been placed here following the restoration necessary after the flood of 1966.

Grouped in one room, therefore, are some of the masterpieces of fifteenth century Florentine sculpture, evidence of its two diverse tendencies: the measured classicism of the choir gallery by Luca della Robbia contrasted with Donatello's free and broad-minded interpretation of the antique.

This room is particularly dedicated to Donatello, with its exceptional selection of some of his most well-known pieces. From the early *Prophets*, the composite joy of the «cantoria» to the tormented plasticity of the *Habakkuk* and the wooden *Magdalene*, one can study his progression towards an emphasis on expressive character, using a wide and varied style, together with enormous technical versatility. Apart from these, the room also contains the statues by Andrea Pisano which form the immediate sequence to the cycle of sculptures dating to the fourteenth century in the adjoining room, which displays the first and second order of the Bell Tower panels.

*The Kings, Sybils and Prophets by Andrea Pisano*

*The Kings and Sybils* date from 1342 to 1343 and are displayed along the wall leading to the stairs. Originally situated on the east side of the Bell Tower (its principal side, aligned with the Cathedral facade), they were substituted by Donatello's *Prophets* in 1464 and transferred to the North side. An iconographical explanation for these statues (in actual fact, high-reliefs with unfinished backs, hidden by the niches) can be found in the inscriptions on the cartouches.

From left to right, they represent the *Tiburtine Sybil, King David, King Solomon* and the *Eritrean Sybil*. Within the iconographic programme of the Bell Tower they refer to the Redemption of Mankind, as predicted in Antiquity. Furthermore, the Sybils are attributed with the prophecy of the rise of Florence.

Although provided with corporal mass, the rhythmic flow of the abundant drapery and the subtlety of the surface detail places these statues within a Gothic context, which is abandoned in the *Prophets*, either by Andrea Pisano or based on his design (Moskowitz is of a different opinion) for the south side of the Bell Tower.

These are situated along the opposite wall, and reveal an increased solidity and regularity in volume, which could be described as «classic», and a renewed attention to Giotto.

They are believed to have been realized in the final years of Andrea's Florentine period before his departure for Pisa in 1343 (or otherwise, during his possible return to Florence after 1348: Becherucci).

Their iconography is uncertain: their position within the iconographic cycle of the Bell Tower, their senile, bearded appearance and the presence of scrolls (even though the figure bearing the tablet has been interpreted as the Patriarch Moses) would lead to their interpretation as Prophets.

*The Prophets by Donatello*

The statues from the east side are now situated on the right wall in their original order. Together with those missing from the north side, they were commissioned from Donatello (1386-1466) between 1415 and 1421. The iconographic theme remained that of the Prophets and the Patriarchs. The age-old debate concerning their date and Donatello's contribution to each of these statues continues today, even though certain dates accompanied by documentary evidence have recently emerged.

68

The first two statues believed completed are the *Beardless Prophet* (1415-'18); perhaps a portrait of his friend, Brunelleschi) for the niche on the extreme left, and the *Bearded Prophet*, known as *il «Pensieroso»* (1418-'20) for the niche on the extreme right. The portrait realism of these two faces provides the two prophetic figures wrapped in the intense concentration of silent meditation with humanity and expressive vitality.

The other figure of a *Bearded Prophet* (next to the beardless one) had previously been attributed to Donatello, but more recently to his collaborator, Nanni di Bartolo, known as «il Rosso». The form of the pentagonal base and the position of the figure itself lead to the almost certain conclusion that it was originally intended for one of the buttresses of the apse of Santa Maria del Fiore. This has, in turn,

caused this statue to be identified with the sculpture of David, which appears from the documents to have been realized by Donatello in 1408-'09 (Bellosi) for that position.

This is followed by the *Sacrifice of Isaac*; documents assign this to Donatello with the help of Nanni di Bartolo and date it to 1421.

The figurative theme, heavy with pathos, had already been interpreted twenty years earlier by both Ghiberti and Brunelleschi in the panels realized for the competition for the door of San Giovanni (1401).

Donatello's version is totally original both in its iconography, representing the moment in which the action is suspended by the appearance of the angel, and in its composition, which develops a series of dynamic tensions in contrast to the upwards movement (a solution necessitated by the narrow space within the niche). Certain weakness in the execution of the body and left arm of Abraham can be attributed to workshop help.

A few years later — between 1425 and 1436 — Donatello began the second series of Prophets, now on the wall facing the above, which were to substitute the fourteenth century series by Andrea Pisano on the West side of the Bell Tower. From the left, the figure identified on the basis of the inscription on the scroll in his hands as *St. John the Evangelist* («Ecce Agnus Dei») repeats the position of the *Beardless Prophet*. This has not been definitely attributed to Donatello. The signature («Donatello») on the base in vernacular is apocryphal and a later addition. It is possibly the work of Nanni di Bartolo.

Following these, two of the most famous works by Donatello: *Habakkuk*, popularly known as the «Zuccone» (1434-'36) and *Jeremiah* (1423-'25). A popular tradition, dating to the sixteenth century (and confirmed by Vasari) maintained that they were portraits of two Medici rivals, Giovanni Chiericini and Francesco Soderini. Although this theory has been negated by the critics, there seems to be some hint of portraiture even to a modern eye in their expressive realism. Realism, therefore, not for its own sake but as an instrument «to express in concrete form the many aspects of human suffering» (Becherucci), concentrated in the prophets of malediction and lamentation.

Habakkuk is represented in the act of shouting out his pleas and dreadful demands concerning the nature of evil. His tunic hangs in one long pleat from the shoulder of his exhausted, ascetic's body. This hollow-cheeked figure, consumed by suffering, prompted the famous anecdote from Vasari, according to which the artist, while working on the sculpture, ordered it with obsessive repetition to talk to him.

Jeremiah, with his ungirt figure, contracted features and lips pursed in an expression of suffering and submission represents the prophet of the exile and destruction of Jerusalem; an object of persecution and derision on account of his prophecies.

The last of the series, the *Prophet Abdia* by Nanni di Bartolo is the only signed Florentine work by this artist (on the cartouche: «Johannes Rossus prophetam me sculpsit Abdiam). Abdia, dating to about 1412, reflects the influence of Donatello, even though revealing at the same time its own personal style in the sinuosity of the lines and the general melancholy of the figure.

70

## The Choir Galleries

With the statues for the Bell Tower yet to be completed and while Brunelleschi was in the process of finishing his dome, Donatello had to compete with the young Luca della Robbia in the construction of the so-called «Cantorie» (choir galleries) of Santa Maria Novella (the marble organ lofts above the sacristies). In 1431 Luca was the first to be entrusted with the *Cantoria* to be situated above the door to the Sacrestia Nuova or «delle Messe», which was finished in 1438; immediately afterwards, in 1433, Donatello received the commission for the other, to be placed above the symmetrical sacristy (called Vecchia or dei Canonici), which was completed in 1440.

The two choir galleries remained in their original positions until 1688, when they were dismantled and in large part removed from Santa Maria del Fiore, in occasion of the magnificent baroque decoration for the wedding of Ferdinando, son of Cosimo III, with Violante Beatrice di Baviera. On this occasion, the still unfinished facade was covered with plaster bricks, and painted with a false facade. This fresco, much faded with time, remained there until the definitive facade was realized. In 1841, the remaining architectural parts of the choir galleries were removed to be replaced with those by the architect, Gaetano Baccani.

The choir galleries as we see them today are the result of a modern reconstruction and integration, which took place simultaneously with their transfer to the Museum.

On the entrance wall (by the stairs) is that by Luca della Robbia. The ten original reliefs, six from the parapet and four from the spaces between the large corbels, are positioned below for better visibility. Illustrating the last psalm of King David (CL), they figure children praising the Lord with song, dance and music.

The verses of the psalm are distributed around the cyma, the base of the parapet and the base of the corbels: «LAUDATE DOMINUM IN SANCTIS EIUS; LAU-

*Donatello, Jeremiah, detail.*

*Luca della Robbia, choir gallery.*

*Donatello, choir gallery.*

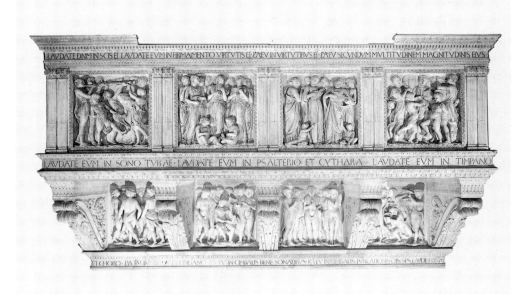

DATE EUM IN FIRMAMENTO VIRTUTIS EIUS/LAUDATE EUM IN VIRTUTIBUS EIUS; LAUDATE EUM SECUNDUM MULTITUDINEM MAGNITUDINIS EIUS (singers with a book; singers with a scroll: sides of the parapet) LAUDATE EUM IN SONO TUBAE; LAUDATE EUM IN PSATERIO ET CYTHARA. LAUDATE EUM IN TIMPANO (trumpet players; psaltery players; lyre players; tambourine players: front of the parapet) ET CHORO; LAUDATE EUM IN CHORDIS ET ORGANO. LAUDATE EUM IN CIMBALIS BENESONANTIBUS; LAUDATE EUM IN CIMBALIS JUBILATONIS OMNIS SPIRITUS LAUDET DOMINUM (dancing putti, organ, harp and lute players, drum and cymbal players, cymbal players: between the corbels)».

The composure of the figures and the grace of their movement is combined with the careful expression of their joyful state of mind (Vasari noted that in certain singers, «one can observe the song swelling in their throat: and the shrugging shoulders of those keeping time with the music»). The strong relief emerges from a smooth background between pairs of flat brunelleschian plaster strips and corbels, richly decorated with vegetable motifs, with which the groups are connected in a simple, clear rhythm. In this first work by Luca della Robbia known to us, the qualities of his art are already expressed: his sense of equilibrium and his serene attitude to life were to be reflected in his limpid and luminous technique of glazing terracotta, in which he later specialized.

On the opposite wall, we find the *Cantoria* by Donatello. The figurative theme is of classical inspiration (dance of the maidens), suggested by the Cathedral constructor, Neri di Gino Capponi and permitted the artist to express his idea in an agitated composition: a continual relief of putti who dance within a narrow space, between the twin columns «a giorno», covered with mosaic, and the mosaic background. The glint of the mosaic against which the white, dancing figures stand out, together with the polychrome of the architectural elements give a light and colourful aspect to this «cantoria». Donatello had been inspired by the similar effect of the facade by Arnolfo for Santa Maria del Fiore and within the dim light of the Cathedral interior, it served to enliven the cross-vault.

Donatello's use of the most disperate antique sources is a typical feature of his work, both for the composition and for the architectural and decorative details. Notwithstanding the heterogeneity of the sources and the naturalistic exuberance, the work is decisively «anti-classical». Even the two bronze heads (originally gilded), within tondi be-

*Donatello, choir gallery, detail.*

*Donatello, choir gallery, detail.*

76

tween the corbels, are perhaps replicas of antique heads (Janson) but their iconographic significance is not very clear. The border of the gallery with alternating vases and acanthus leaves is a nineteenth century reconstruction.

Donatello's iconographic solutions, both architectural and decorative, are evidently quite different from those of Luca. Furthermore, the modelling technique used for the figures is quite distinct: the *cantorie* were positioned far from the viewer's eye, high up above the sacristy doors, in the dim light of the church's interior, and Vasari, noting the greater effect of Donatello's unfinished («in bozze») treatment of the surfaces, established the now traditional comparison with the excessive «finish and polish» of those of Luca della Robbia. Vasari's observation («a burst of fury in art will express a soul's concept, never achieved with the diligence and hard work of the highly finished») in his *Lives of the Artists* introduces his reader to an appreciation of the michelangelesque incomplete.

### The Magdalene by Donatello

Beneath Donatello's cantoria is his wooden figure of *Mary Magdalene*. In the absence of documented information, this sculpture has been dated on the basis of stylistic analysis to the artist's late phase,

around 1455, after his return from Padova. It was probably destined for the Baptistry, where it is recorded up to the sixteenth century.

The Maddalena is unusually portrayed in her old age, «consumed by fasting and abstinence» (Vasari) and can be compared with other figures of penitent and ascetic saints by Donatello, in particular the bronze figure of *St. John the Baptist* in the Cathedral of Siena.

Her body is portrayed in the moment of its physical decline and becomes the means of expressing a psychic force through its dignity and spiritual tension in the act of prayer. Its intimate vitality is accented by a technique which consumes the form; it is brought alive by the passage of light over its surfaces and hard-edged outlines, typical of wooden sculptures. Donatello increased this expressive effect by modelling many of the details in malleable materials (stubble and plaster) and then painting the figure with very naturalistic colours, even highlighting the hair with touches of gold.

On the end walls of this room, above, are *two tapestries* dating to the end of the sixteenth century and originating from the Medici workshops. Based on designs by Alessandro Allori, they represent, on the left, *Zachariah blessing St. John* (bearing the inscription «Ante Faciem Domini») and, on the right, *Zachariah writing the name of the Baptist* (with the inscription: «Vitate Eius gaudebunt»).

In the little passage way leading to the Room of the Silver Altar: two panels with a series of modern *medallions and cones*, commemorating the facade of Santa Maria del Fiore and the Baptistry; two wooden panels displaying on one, *a flattened piece of organ pipe from the Cathedral* with the inscription «Cosmo Med. Rep. Flor. duce II Bernardi Argenti ord. pred. opus. 1546», on the other, *six measures for wood for ship masts* (1615) originating from the Casentine forest, formerly property of the Opera del Duomo. Underneath these panels, a display case containing *four types of forest hammer* for the marking of wood (second half of the eighteenth century).

### 15. The Room of the Silver Altar

This room, containing the silver altar-frontal and the cross of San Giovanni, was first opened together with the Museum itself in 1891. At present, it also contains other works from the Baptistry; from the embroideries of the vestments of San Giovanni Battista to the very precious mosaic diptych with the Christian festivities and the gilded panels for the famous Porta del Paradiso by Lorenzo Ghiberti,

*Donatello, Magdalene.*

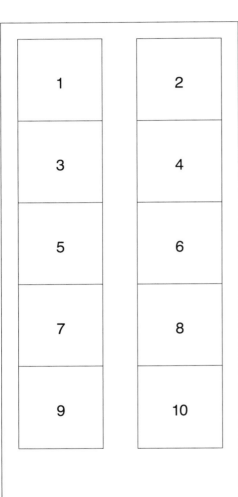

1. Adam and Eve
2. Cain and Abel
3. Noah
4. Abraham
5. Isaac
6. Joseph
7. Moses
8. Joshua
9. Saul and David
10. Solomon

which have recently been restored and subsequently transferred to the Museum (1985-'86 circa). The chronological context remains that of the fifteenth century, represented by the so-called «minor arts», which, at the time were «the most active field of experience, which nourished the renewal (of the arts) and were the apprenticeship for the major artists» (Becherucci, in Becherucci-Brunetti). They also reflected an exceptionally refined society of enormous economic potential at the height of its splendour.

On the walls, the relatively small collection of paintings, which originally hung in Santa Maria del Fiore and which have remained in Florence, dating from the end of the thirteenth to the beginning of the fifteenth centuries.

*The panels from the Porta del Paradiso*

In the centre of the room, within a custom built display case (with an inert atmosphere dehumidifier), are the first *two panels* from the *Porta del Paradiso* to be restored following damage undergone during the flood of 1966 (the removal of the other eight panels is in process and for conservation reasons, they will also be transferred to the Museum of the Opera del Duomo).

The so-called «Porta del Paradiso» was the third door in chronological order to be realized for the Baptistry of San Giovanni.

It was commissioned in 1425 with no competition, by the Merchant's Guild (patron and sponsor of the Baptistry) from Lorenzo Ghiberti. He had already successfully completed the door (now on the north side) figuring stories from the New Testament following a competition in 1401. (The first of the three bronze doors, dedicated to San Giovanni Battista, was realized by Andrea Pisano and positioned on the east front in 1338; it is at present to be found on the west side).

At the end of his second *Commentario*, concerning the door, Ghiberti writes: «I was given the freedom to create a work which I considered to be the most perfect, the most ornate and the most rich». Indeed after thirty years of projection and hard work both by Ghiberti and his collaborators (his sons, Vittore and Tommasso, Benozzo Gozzoli, Bernardo Cellini and others), on account of its beauty the door was mounted in 1452 in the place of honour, on the east side, before the main entrance to the Cathedral: the «Paradisius» according to liturgical tradition. Vasari then rendered this name famous with his anecdote in which Michelangelo judged this work worthy of Paradise.

Quite apart from its religious importance, the civic and social significance of the door's project was underlined by the choice of Leonardo Bruni, the humanist Chancellor of the Florentine Republic, as formulator of the elaborate, iconographical programme, which was to be dedicated to the Old Testament. In actual fact, the compositive scheme proposed by Bruni underwent radical changes; it seems that it was substituted by the proposal of Ambrogio Traversari, the General of the Order of the Camaldolesi, and friend of Cosimo il Vecchio (Krautheimer) or, as has been recently suggested, that taken from the *Summa Theologica* by Sant'Antonino, Bishop of Florence (Hartt).

In contrast to the two older doors, divided into twenty panels (as foreseen in Bruni's project), the entire biblical cycle of the Porta del Paradiso is divided into only ten panels (five for each side); each panel includes various scenes.

The two panels on display are dedicated to the *Stories of Saul and David* (facing the entrance to the room), originally the bottom panel of the left door, and the *Story of Joseph*, located at the centre of the right hand door. This last, which Vasari maintained «for a number of reasons... to be the most deserving, the most difficult and the most beautiful», includes various scenes taken from Genesis, intelligently composed within an imposing architectural structure in perspective and with a wealth of detail. Following the sequence of events in the Bible, the panels represents: above right, Joseph taken from the well and sold by his brothers to the Ishmaelite merchants travelling towards Egypt. Within a large round building, the principal scene takes place: the storage of the grain crops in the granaries of Egypt in preparation for the famine, foreseen by Joseph in the dream of the Pharoah. The story continues to the left (below) with the discovery of Joseph's cup in Benjamin's sack. Above, Joseph reveals his identity to his brothers and embraces Benjamin, while another brother kneels before his feet. Finally, the last episode at the bottom right, of less certain identification, could represent either the distribution of the grain and the gifts to the brothers of Joseph or their return to their father.

The biblical content of these stories, which aims to emphasize Joseph's role as the prefigurator of the message of God's salvation, is linked to allusions about contemporary political and social life: the images of the wealth and plenty in Egypt were probably intended to exalt Florentine prosperity under the new government of Cosimo il Vecchio,

who had returned from exile in 1434 (Ciardi Dupré).

The panel with the *Stories of Saul and David* has a very different composition in part due to its intended position with respect to the observer. The episodes, taken from the first book of Samuel, are much less clearly identifiable: the entire foreground is dedicated to a battle, full of action, between the Philistines and the army of Israel, lead by Saul in imperial dress and commanding attitude; in the centre, David decapitates Goliath. A landscape fills the background, and on the horizon, the city of Jerusalem (an idealized version of Florence) towards which the victorious David turns, bearing the head of Goliath.

The combination of many scenes in one panel provides a rich narrative content, even though the compositive scheme is extremely simple. A new sculptural concept is involved here, mainly realized through the use of so-called narrative relief. This consists of a gradual flattening of the volumes (varying from high-and low-relief to «stiacciato») and a progressive decrease in the height of the figures and the objects towards the background. The rules of the new perspective, developed by Brunelleschi, Donatello and Masaccio, have clearly been applied here, even though they do not achieve a totally organic and unitarian whole. The viewer's attention is still drawn to details, which in their tiniest parts reveal a vast cultural preparation.

«It is the most remarkable work of art that I have produced: in order to complete it, I have used every art, measure and faculty», Ghiberti himself commented on the Porta del Paradiso. He was aware that he had reached the highest peak in his art, and indeed in his specialized technique of casting bronze, introduced to Florence by the Venetian maestro Lorenzo d'Avanzo (active in the first half of the fourteenth century). The most striking evidence of this was the gilded surface of both doors.

The gold patina, darkened over the centuries to the point of being forgotten, was revealed again following an initial restoration in 1946-'48 (the door had been removed from the Baptistry during the war), but continued to be exposed to harmful atmospheric agents, quite apart from suffering severe damage during the disastrous flooding of the Arno (1966). Subsequent to recent restoration, the two panels displayed here can finally be appreciated in all their splendour, even though they lose much of their original significance in the ascetic setting of the museum.

On a shelf in front of these two panels (against the

*Lorenzo Ghiberti, panel for the Porta del Paradiso with the stories of Saul and David.*

*Lorenzo Ghiberti, panel for the Porta del Paradiso
with the stories of Joseph.*

82

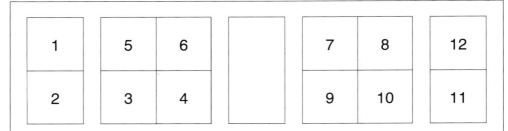

1. The Annunciation to Zachariah and the Visitation
2. The birth of St. John
3. St. John in the desert
4. St. John preaches to the rabble
5. Christ visits St. John in the desert
6. The Baptism of Christ
7. St. John baptizes the people
8. Christ receives the messengers of St. John
9. St. John before Herod
10. St. John visited by the disciples in prison
11. The decapitation of St. John
12. Herod's banquet

end wall), the silver altar-frontal and cross from the Baptistry. Their significant position within the Museum reflects their original location facing the Porta del Paradiso.

## The Silver Altar-Frontal of San Giovanni

The completion of this Florentine goldsmith's masterpiece stretched over more than a century, from 1366 to 1480. The twelve reliefs representing the life of Saint John the Baptist — eight on the front and two on the sides — are positioned within an elaborate, architectural structure, late Gothic in style, with polygonal pilasters decorated with statues within niches, repeated as decoration on the upper part. In the centre, the tabernacle is surmounted by a statue of the Baptist.

The silver altar-frontal with translucent enamelling and gilding (total weight of the silver: 396 Kg. circa), was commissioned by the powerful Merchant's Guild, which was at that time patron of the Baptistry (at the bottom, against a cobalt blue enamelled background, an inscription recalls the names of the Guild officials, who were responsible for the commission, and the date the work was begun: «Anno domini MCCCLXVI inceptum fuit hoc opus dessalis tenpore Benedicti Nerozzi de Albertis Pauli Michaelis de Rondinellis Bernardi Domini Chovonis de Chovonibus offitialium deputatorum) and was intended to cover and protect the high altar of the Baptistry of San Giovanni. Such a project was not totally innovative in Tuscany; a similarly imposing and precious work had already been made for the Cathedral of Pistoia.

Documents have provided the names of those goldsmiths who completed the front section during the last decade of the fourteenth century: Leonardo di Ser Giovanni, Betto di Geri, Cristofano di Paolo and Michele di Monte. Of those nominated, other works have only been attributed to Leonardo di Ser Giovanni and the task of attributing sections to each artist has therefore proved difficult and complex; indeed, research is still in process. It can however be confirmed that all the front reliefs are related to the orcagnesque tradition which dominated the Florentine artistic scene for at least the whole of the second half of the fourteenth century. The valuable silver statuette, partly gilded, was positioned in the central space in 1452. Representing St. John the Baptist, it is the work of sculptor and architect, Michelozzo Michelozzi, who adhered to the style of the earlier parts of the frontal.

It is probable that at the same time, the frontal was moved from its original position, as an ornament for the high altar, and was situated in the centre of the Baptistry, above the font, where it was used to display the treasures of San Giovanni in occasion of the feast days of the Baptist and the Perdono (13th

*Florentine «maestri» of 14th and 15th centuries,
the altar-frontal of San Giovanni.*

January: the feast day of the Baptism of Christ). It thus became «the symbolic altar of all that which religious history, together with civic history, had accumulated in the church, the spiritual centre of Florence» (Becherucci).

Between 1477 and 1480, the four lateral reliefs were realized by Bernardo Cennini, Antonio del Pollaiolo, Andrea del Verrocchio, two of the major contemporary artists, and Antonio di Salvi Salvucci with the help of Francesco di Giovanni. On the left side the relief by Bernardo Cennini (above) unites two episodes in a single composition; the *Annunciation to Zachariah* and the *Visitation*, against a background of refined architecture. *The Nativity of St. John the Baptist* by Antonio del Pollaiolo is an interior scene with a realistic and spontaneous atmosphere, animated by the elegant, rhythmic flow of the lines.

On the right side, the *Beheading of St. John* by Verrocchio (below) in a setting of arched architecture. The lively composition, in which Pollaiolo's influence is evident, includes two groups of figures around the central scene of the beheading of the Baptist, displaying very different emotions; from the disturbed agitation of the figures on the left to the brusque violence of the two characters on the right. *Herod's Banquet* (above) is the only work to be definitely attributed to Antonio di Salvi Salvucci, who appears however to be a "minor" artist from

his version of the Pollaiolesque model lacking expressive energy.

The carved and gilded wooden frame, above and below the altar frontal, could have been added at the end of the fifteenth century.

*The Silver Cross*

The great cross, like the altar-frontal, was commissioned by the Merchant's Guild. The work was realized between 1457 and 1459; the upper part by Betto di Francesco Betti and the lower part by Miliano di Domenico Dei (?) and Antonio del Pollaiolo. The precise information provided by written documents has not however convinced the critics, who believe that the Crucifix, together with the two lateral statuettes of St. John the Baptist and the Madonna do not belong to the Cross (the attributions vary; we note here Becherucci's attribution to Bernardo Cennini, 1415-'98, and that of Parronchi to Luca della Robbia, 1400-'82). Not only these three figures, but the attribution and date of every single part of this work of art has been discussed at length, without, however, reaching any positive conclusions.

The original function of the cross is also uncertain. It seems that it was intended as a case for the holy relic of the wood from the Cross, which had been in the possession of the Merchant's Guild since ancient times (according to the legend, it was donated to

*Bernardo Cennini, the Announcement to Zaccariah and the Visitation - Antonio del Pollaiolo, the Nativity of the Baptist. Left side of the altar-frontal.*

*Antonio di Salvi and Francesco di Giovanni, Herod's Banquet - Andrea del Verrocchio, the Decapitation of the Baptist. Right side of the altar-frontal.*

Florence by Carlo Magno). The reliquary had also to be shown to its best advantage, as it was in direct competition with a similar one which appeared in Florence in 1454 and was bought the following year by the Wool Guild for Santa Maria del Fiore. Already, in the 1470's, the cross must have lost its function as a reliquary and as a consequence, its proportions were also changed (it was at this time that the Crucifix and the two statuettes of St. John the Baptist and the Madonna were added) in order for it to be displayed on the silver altar-frontal of the Baptistry on the feast days of Santo Patrono and of the Perdono as the altar cross, or as the monstrance for the same reliquary (Parronchi adds that the cross was used as a reliquary).

The iconographic theme seems to have been organically conceived in two distinct cycles, one on the cross itself and the other on the stem and the base. The cross is dedicated to the Sacrifice of Christ as the central event in the Salvation of Mankind and is decorated with elaborate enamelling (*recto*: within the mixtilinear compasses at the ends of the arms, the *Eternal Father* (above), the *Virgin* (left), the *Apostle John* (right) and the *Magdalene* (below); at the cross itself, the Pelican, symbol of extreme sacrifice and half way down the lesser arm, a *Saint. Verso*: the *Agnus Dei* at the crossing of the arms, surrounded by *Prophets* and perhaps a *Sybil*, in the compasses at the ends of the arms, the four *Evangelists*, halfway down the lesser arm, *St. John the Baptist in the Desert*). The cross is removable and fixed to a support with a relief representing Calvary with a skull, surrounded by the image of Jerusalem. Immediately below this support, two tondi figuring the *Saints* and the *Annunciation* and the two lateral arms which sustain the statuettes of the Virgin and St. John the Baptist.

The lower part of the cross is dedicated to St. John the Baptist, Precursor of the Redemption and titular of the Baptistery, who is seated in majesty flanked by two adoring angels in the central temple-shaped aedicola, obviously influenced by Brunelleschi. The lobed base is decorated with reliefs of the *Baptism of Christ*, the *Fathers of the Church, Moses* and the *Theological Virtues*, two *Angels* and various emblems of the Merchant's Guild. On the sides, two supports in the form of sphinxes sustain two angels in full relief.

The exceptional importance of the silver altar-frontal and cross lies in the complexity of its iconography and the importance of the artists involved. It stands as one of the most significant examples of Florentine art dating from this period.

*Attributed to Giovanni del Biondo, The Martyrdom
of San Sebastiano, central part of the triptych.*

86

## The Vestments of the San Giovanni

Another important Florentine work of art from the second half of the fifteenth century is the *set of vestments for the Holy Mass* (two dalmatics, a chasuble and a cope), commissioned from the Merchant's Guild for the Baptistry of San Giovanni. The remaining twenty seven embroidered squares with the stories of St. John the Baptist are to be found in the two long display cases along the lateral walls (they are glued to panels and framed; at present two are in restoration at the Opificio delle Pietre Dure di Firenze). The work, realized in successive stages between 1466 and 1480 was entrusted to one of the greatest contemporary artists, Antonio del Pollaiolo (1443 circa-1498) who had already worked on the silver altar-frontal, and some of the most expert master embroiderers (Paolo di Bartolomeo da Verona, Coppino di Giovanni di Malines di Fiandra, Piero di Piero da Venezia, Paolo di Bartolomeo da Verona, Niccolò di Jacopo di Francia, Antonio di Giovanni da Firenze): the only two Italians were a Florentine and a Venetian. The sophisticated embroidery techniques (or "nué") using polychrome silks woven between fine horizontally stretched golden thread with tiny, subtle stitches, managed to render the modelled chiaroscuro, the intense vitality and expressive variety of Pollaiolo's work.

Apart from the refined design and technique, the iconography is significant: the figurative cycle includes every detail of St. John the Baptist's life (*Visitation; the Birth of the Baptist is announced to Zachariah; the Birth of the Baptist; Zachariah writing the name of the Baptist; the Circumcision of the Baptist; the Baptist encounters the Customs Authorities; the Baptist rebukes Herod; the Baptism of the Converts; the Baptist preaches to the rabble; the Meeting between the Baptist and the Great Priest; the Baptist before the Priest and Levites; Zachariah leave the Temple, the Baptist announces Christ's mission to the Pharisees; the Baptist shows Christ to the People; the Meeting of the Baptist with the Redeemer; Jesus baptizes the Baptist; the Baptist is accused by Herod's wife; the Arrest of the Baptist; the Baptist is conducted to Prison; the Baptist is visited in prison by the Disciples; the Dance of Salome; the Decapitation of the Baptist; the Presentation of the Head of the Baptist to Herod's wife; Herod's Banquet; the Transport of the Body of St. John; the Burial of the Baptist; the Descent into Limbo*). The work was displayed to the faithful on feast days in the centre of the Baptistry on the silver altar-frontal.

## Paintings, mosaics and sculpture

Along the walls of this room are hung the paintings which originally decorated the altars and chapels inside the Cathedral and which remained in the possession of the Opera. Almost all the Cathedral paintings were systematically dispersed from the fifteenth century onwards, when contemporary taste no longer appreciated their simplicity and iconic solemnity. Furthermore, they were no longer adapted to the organic and unitary space, created by the completion of the cupola, in which they were a dispersive force.

On the entrance wall, from the left: *San Zanobi and one of his faithful* (above: *the Annunciation*) with the mighty figure of the Saint, Bishop and Patron Saint of Florence, in a wide red cope, by Jacopo di Cione (active in the second half of the fourteenth century), brother to the two artists Andrea and Nardo Orcagna, with whom he shared the same stylistic tendencies; *Tryptich of San Sebastiano* by an artist linked to the Orcagna workshop but

*Antonio del Pollaiolo, embroidered vestment, detail.*

*Antonio del Pollaiolo, embroidered vestment, detail.*

*Attributed to Jacopo della Quercia,*
*the Announcing Angel.*

*Attributed to Jacopo della Quercia,*
*the Virgin Announced.*

characterized by his bright chromatic range (attributed to Giovanni del Biondo: active 1356-'98). The Martyrdom of San Sebastiano is represented in the central section in the cusp, the head of Christ in the act of benediction, bearing an open book with the symbols of Eternity; to the sides, four stories from the life of the Saint and the Annunciation. From the same artistic background, but later (beginning of the fifteenth century), the following painting, badly damaged and badly retrouched, of *Santa Reparata and the stories of her martyrdom*: the Saint in the centre bears the standard with the Florentine Cross of the People (red on white background), a book and a martyr's palm, flanked by four stories of her martyrdom and of the patron Saints of Florence, St. John the Baptist and San Zanobi.

Above the display case containing the vestments of San Giovanni, there is a group of sculptural works, originating from the Baptistry: two marble fragments with *crowned female busts*, which are attributed to the Sienese sculptor Tino da Camaino, in the last stage of his Florentine phase (1321-'25); they are a part of the group of statues which were originally situated above one of the doors to the Florentine Baptistry. The iconography would seem to correspond to the Theological Virtues, Faith and Charity (with the cornucopia). Between the two busts, there is a polychrome wooden *cross*, which comes from the altar to the right of the Porta del Paradiso in the Baptistry. The movable arms are an unusual characteristic linked to the liturgical necessity of representing the deposition from the cross and the entombment on Good Friday. The intense dramatic expression of this image combines with the refined workmanship of the anatomy and the details. It is attributed to Giovanni di Balduccio (active 1317-'49) and dated to the years immediately before his departure for Milan in 1334 (Lisner). To the left and the right of the silver altar, above the steps, there are respectively the *Angel of the Annunciation* and its *pendant, the Virgin Announced*. The two marble statues were realized in about 1397 for the lunette of the Porta della Mandorla on the North side of Santa Maria del Fiore, but they were not positioned until 1414. They were then substituted by the mosaic *Annunciation* by Domenico and David del Ghirlandaio, which can still be seen in position today (1489).

The dominating features in these statues are their classical sense, both in their solid, composed forms, and in their Apollonian expression of the Angel and the Virgin, who is unusually represented with short

hair, like «the winner of an Olympic medal» (Marchini); a precedent of a tendency which was to develop fully some decades later in the work of Nanni di Banco and Donatello. A credible hypothesis is the attribution to the young Sienese sculptor, Jacopo della Quercia whose activity in Florence before his participation in the competition for the second door for the Baptistry in 1401 is documented (Vasari), but the attribution to Nanni di Banco should not be underestimated (Francovich, Planiscig, Galassi).

On the wall to the left of the silver alter, a marble bas-relief with *the Madonna and Child*, which Vasari states as already being in the old offices of the Magistratura dell'Opera del Duomo (around the middle of the sixteenth century) and which he attributes to Pagno di Lapo Portigiani (1408-'70). Although this attribution has been accepted both by past and recent criticism, very recently it has been doubted, and, amongst others, the names of Agostino di Duccio (Janson) and Antonio Rossellino

*Attributed to Giovanni del Biondo,*
*Santa Caterina d'Alessandria and stories of her life.*

daio, Sandro Botticelli, Monte and Gherardo di Giovanni) following the wish of Lorenzo il Magnifico and interrupted at his death. Even though the work on the chapel was never finished, this model by Monte, which had won the competition against David del Ghirlandaio, was provided with a gilded wood frame (which it still retains) and became an object of popular devotion. The custom of its display in the middle of the Cathedral on the feast day of the Saint continued until its transfer to the newly-founded Museum in 1891.

Descending the stairs, there follows a painting in tempera on canvas of *the Decapitation of the Baptist* (lined with canvas and mounted on a wooden framework). Originally this must have been a processional banner (or a gonfalon) and it shows signs of wear, typical of this type of object. Considered to be Florentine, dating to the beginning of the fifteenth century (Brunetti, in Becherucci-Brunetti), it has recently been attributed to Antonio Veneziano (Bonsanti, 1985, and Ladis) in his last phase, which reveals the beginning of the international Gothic in the treatment of the expression and the naturalistic elements.

Beyond the display case with the embroidery of the vestments of San Giovanni, there are another *two vestment fragments* united in one frame. The embroidery is in silk and gold with larger stitches than those following Pollaiolo's design and appears to be later, both in technique and style (16th century). They probably represent two apparitions of Christ after the Resurrection to the Virgin and to the apostle Peter. Above, a marble statue of a crowned *Santa Reparata* bearing the martyr's palm, *pendant* to the similar statue of the *Redeemer in the act of blessing,* further along the same wall. Both of these are attributed to Andrea Pisano and date to the year he began his collaboration with Giotto on the Bell Tower, about 1335.

The collection of paintings continues with two works of unknown provenance: *Sant'Ivo*, the patron saint of lawyers, notaries and judges, represented here with a woman offering a scroll and a man with a money bag. This can be dated to the second half of the fifteenth century even though the cuspidated frame and the gold ground are typically fourteenth century. Following this, the tryptich with *St. John the Baptist between San Zanobi and Santa Reparata* attributed to the «Maestro of the polyptich of the Medici Chapel».

The last two paintings on this wall come from Santa Maria del Fiore: the *Madonna suckling her Child between St. John the Baptist and San Biagio* is

(Brunetti, in Becherucci-Brunetti) have been assigned to this Madonna, absorbed in melancholy thought.

On the opposite wall, to the right of the altar, *the bust of San Zanobi in the act of benediction* in a mosaic of gilt and polychrome glass paste squares. This was a model commissioned by the Opera del Duomo in 1504 from Monte di Giovanni, also famous for his miniatures, in competition with that of David del Ghirlandaio, in order to decide which artist should be entrusted with the mosaic decoration for the Chapel of San Zanobi (in the centre of the middle apse). This project had been commenced in 1491 (by Domenico and David del Ghirlan-

*The Maestro del Bigallo, San Zanobi between the Saints Eugenio and Crescenzio and stories of his life.*

Florentine, dating to the second half of the fourteenth century. Its position within the Cathedral changed many times and it was an object of popular devotion. Next to this, the *Santa Caterina d'Alessandria* (and stories of her life) was realized in two stages; the original part is attributed to Giovanni del Biondo (the central cuspidated panel with Santa Caterina and the portrait of the donor at her feet) and another part, attributed to Giovanni del Ponte (including the other two donors below, the triangles above bearing the images of San Bartolomeo to the left and St. John the Baptist to the right and the lateral stories with the life of the Saint).

The inscription below on the frame includes the names of the three patrons figured in the painting: «Questi sono N(ofer)o Bischeri Messere B(artolomeo) e G(iovanni) suoi figliuoli», between two coats-of-arms, the one on the left belonging to the Bischeri family, the one on the right not identifiable. Noferi Bischeri was in influential citizen and Consul of the Wool Guild (patron of Santa Maria del Fiore) from 1378, the year in which this work was probably realized. The painting was perhaps enlarged for the occasion and was placed in the private chapel of the same Nofero Bischeri, which he founded in the Florentine Cathedral in 1407.

On the right wall, in the centre, a thirteenth century panel with the much venerated effigy of *San Zanobi (between the Deacon Saints Eugenio and Crescenzio) with the stories of his life*. Popular belief maintains that this was painted on the wood of an elm tree which flowered miraculously in the piazza di San Giovanni, when the body of the Saint was transferred from the church of San Lorenzo to the Cathedral of Santa Reparata (the inscription between the Saint and the Deacon Eugenio reads: This panel was made from the elm of the Piazza. January CCCCXXVIIII). A singular work, much damaged and heavily repainted until its recent restoration and cleaning (1937; however, there remains no trace of the original version of the fifteenth century face of the Saint), it contains very differing characteristics: the precious and elongated stylization of the Byzantine figures is combined with a taste for the narrative and a sense of the plastic, which is typically Florentine. It is believed to be the work of the *Maestro del Bigallo* (the name being derived from the *Crucifix* in the Museum of the Bigallo) and dates to halfway through the thirteenth century.

The Opera's collection of paintings also includes the *processional panel with Sant'Agata* at present (1988) undergoing restoration. The image of the Saint appears on both sides: the earlier one attributed to the so-called «Maestro di Sant'Agata», represents one of the most significant example of byzantine painting dating to the middle of the thirteenth century; the other to Jacopo del Casentino, active in the first half of the fourteenth century.

Beneath the panel with San Zanobi a display case contains the precious couple of *mosaic panels* featuring scenes commemorating the twelve Christian feast days. They are of the most refined technique using miniscule «tessera» in gold, lapislazuli and glass. Originally, they were united in the form of a dyptich, donated to the Basilica of San Giovanni in 1394, together with certain reliquaries of Saints, by a Venetian noblewomen, Madonna Nicoletta Grioni. They are considered to have originated from Constantinople, since the latter was

*Byzantine mosaic panel, 14th century.*

*Byzantine mosaic panel, 14th century.*

*Byzantine mosaic panel, 14th century,*
*detail with the Annunciation.*

the wife of Pietro Torrigiani, a Florentine who was
the secretary to the Emperor of Constantinople,
Giovanni Catacuzeno.

The two little panels have a simple frame in gilded
wood (late fifteenth century), on the back of which
is painted the eagle bearing the bale (of bound
goods) of the Merchant's Guild, patron of San
Giovanni, for display on the silver altar of the
Baptistry during solemn festivals.

At the end of the walls, above the shelves, two
*polychrome terracotta busts*, to the left that of *Santa
Maria Maddalena*, by Giovanni Bandini, known as
dell'Opera, and to the right that of the *Redeemer*,
Florentine art dating to the fifteenth century. Above, in the centre, a fragment of a statue of *Christ in
the act of Blessing*; this, together with the head of St.
John the Baptist, (see p.   ) is all that remains of the
group of the Baptism of Christ by the Sienese Tino
di Camaino dating to 1316-'17, which was originally situated above the south door of the Baptistry.

Above the entrance, a polychrome glazed terracotta
lunette with *Santa Maria Maddalena* against a
landscape attributed to Benedetto Buglioni.

Plan of the ground floor          Plan of the first floor

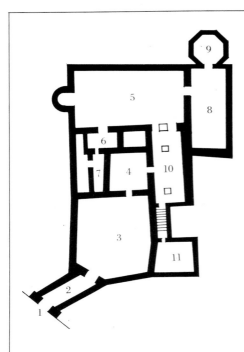
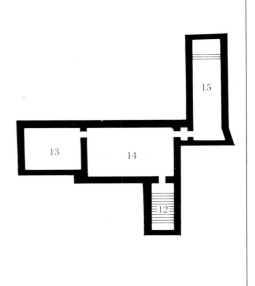

1. Entrance
2. Lobby
3. Courtyard
4. Vestibule
5. Room of the Cathedral Facade
6. Passage
7. Brunelleschi Rooms
8. Room of the Choral Books
9. Chapel
10. Entrance Hall
11. Mezzanine

12. Stairs
13. Room of the Bell-Tower Panels
14. Room of the Choir Galleries
15. Room of the Silver Altar

(Rossi U.), *Catalogo del Museo di Santa Maria del Fiore*, I edizione, Firenze, 1891.

Poggi G., *Catalogo del Museo dell'Opera del Duomo*, II edizione, Firenze, 1904.

Rossi F., *Catalogo del Museo di Santa Maria del Fiore*, III edizione, Firenze, 1964.

Becherucci L. - Brunetti G., *Il Museo dell'Opera del Duomo a Firenze*, voll. 2, Milano, 1969-1970.

Settesoldi E., *Museo dell'Opera del Duomo*, Firenze, 1982.

AA.VV., *Due granduchi tre re e una facciata*, exhibition catalogue, Firenze, 1987.

AA.VV., *Lorenzo Ghiberti: «materia e ragionamenti»*, exhibition catalogue, Firenze, 1978.

AA.VV., *Lorenzo Ghiberti nel suo tempo*, proceedings of the international congress (Firenze 1978), voll. 2, Firenze, 1980.

AA.VV., *La Pittura in Italia. Il Duecento e il Trecento*, 2 vls., Milano, 1986.

Baldini U., *L'opera completa di Michelangelo scultore*, Milano, 1973.

Beck J., *Le porte del Battistero di Firenze*, Firenze, 1985.

Bonsanti C., *Uno stendardo di Antonio Veneziano*, in «Paragone», XXXVI, n. 419, 1985, pp. 53-56.

Bonsanti G. - Darr A.P., *Donatello e i suoi. Scultura fiorentina del primo Rinascimento*, exhibition catalogue (Firenze 1986), Milano, 1986.

Brunetti G., *Il Museo dell'Opera di Santa Maria del Fiore. Luci e ombre dei Musei fiorentini*, in «Atti della Società Leonardo da Vinci», 6, 1975, pp. 19-32.

Brunetti G., *I bassorilievi di Girolamo Ticciati per il coro e per l'altare maggiore del Battistero*, in «Kunst des Barock in der Toskana. Studien zur Kunst unter den letzten Medici» italienische Forschungen IX, 1976, München, pp. 182-187.

Burresi M.G., *Andrea, Nino e Tommaso Pisani*, Milano, 1983.

Carapelli G., Cozzi M., Cresti C., *Il Duomo di Firenze 1822-1847. L'avventura della facciata*, Firenze, 1987.

Ciardi Duprè Del Poggetto M.G., *L'oreficeria nella Firenze del Quattrocento*, exhibition catalogue, Firenze, 1977.

Condivi A., *Vita di Michelangelo Buonarroti* (Roma, 1553), Firenze, 1927, engl. trans. Oxford, 1976.

Diana N., *La cupola di Santa Maria del Fiore in Firenze*, Firenze, 1976.

Garzelli A., *Miniatura fiorentina del Rinascimento (1440-1525). Un primo censimento*, 2 vls., Firenze, 1985.

Gentilini G., *I cartoni di Agostino e Giovanni Lessi per le cantorie di Donatello e di Luca della Robbia*, Firenze, 1984.

Guasti C., *La cupola di Santa Maria del Fiore*, Firenze, 1857.

Guasti C., *Santa Maria del Fiore*, Firenze, 1887.

Hartt F., *Michelangelo's three Pieta's*, New York, 1975.

100

Hartt F., *Lucerna Ardens et Lucens. Il significato della Porta del Paradiso*, in *Lorenzo Ghiberti e il suo tempo*, proceedings of the international congress (Firenze 1978), voll. 2, Firenze, 1980, I, pp. 27-57.

Heykamp D., *Baccio Bandinelli nel Duomo di Firenze*, in «Paragone», n. 175, 1964, pp. 32-42.

Janson H.W., *The Sculpture of Donatello*, II ed., 2 vls., Princeton, 1963.

Krautheimer R., *Lorenzo Ghiberti*, II ed., 2 vls., Princeton, N.J., 1970.

Kreytenberg. G., *Der Campanile von Giotto*, mitteilungen des Kunsthistorischen Institutes in Florenz, XXII, 2, 1978.

Manetti A., *Vita di Filippo Brunelleschi*, (Firenze, 1465 ca.) Milano, 1976.

Marchini G., *Il Battistero, il Duomo e il Museo dell'Opera di Firenze*, Firenze, 1972.

Marchini G., *La cupola: medievale e no*, in *Filippo Brunelleschi. La sua opera il suo tempo*, proceedings of the international congress, 2 vls., Firenze, 1980, pp. 915-920.

Lisner M., *Holzkruzifixe in Florenz und in der Toskana, von der zeit um 1300 bit zum frühen Cinquecento*, München, pp. 22-23.

Matteoli A., *I modelli lignei dal '500 al '600 per la facciata del Duomo di Firenze*, in «Commentari», I-II, 1974, pp. 73-110.

Moskowitz A.F., *Trecento Classicism and the Campanile hexagons*, in «GESTA», XXII, 1, 1983, pp. 49-65.

Moskowitz A.F., *The sculpture of Andrea and Nino Pisano*, Cambridge, 1986, pp. 31-50.

Paolucci A., *Per Cosimo Merlini il vecchio orafo granducale*, in «Antichità Viva», XIV, n. 6, 1975, pp. 24-30.

Paronchi A., *La croce d'argento dell'altare di San Giovanni*, in *Lorenzo Ghiberti nel suo tempo*, proceedings of the international congress (Firenze 1978), voll. 2, 1980, I, pp. 195-217.

Parronchi A., *Sulla Pietà fiorentina di Michelangelo*, in «Michelangelo», 10, 1981, 36-37, pp. 23-35.

Peri P., *Parato composto da un paliotto e una pianeta*, in *Tesori d'Arte dell'Annunziata di Firenze*, exhibition catalogue, Firenze, 1987.

Pope-Hennesy J., *Luca della Robbia*, Oxford, N.Y., 1980.

Pope-Hennesy J., *Donatello*, Oxford-New York, 1985.

Saalman H., *Filippo Brunelleschi. The Cupola of Santa Maria del Fiore*, London 1980.

Sanpaolesi P., *La lanterna di Santa Maria del Fiore e il suo modello ligneo*, in «Bollettino d'Arte del Ministero P.I.», XLI, 1956, pp. 11-29.

Sanpaolesi P., *La cupola di Santa Maria del Fiore. Il progetto. La costruzione*, Firenze, 1977.

Settesoldi E., *Le facciate di Santa Maria del Fiore*, in *Due granduchi tre re e una facciata*, exhibition catalogue, Firenze, 1987.

Toesca P., *Il Trecento*, Torino, 1951.

Trachtemberg M., *The Campanile of Florence Cathedral*, New York, 1971.

Vasari G., *Le Vite de' più eccellenti pittori, scultori, architettori*, ed. G. Milanesi, 9 vls., Firenze, 1878-1885; engl. trans., 3 vls., New York, 1979.

Vasari G., *La Vita di Michelangelo nelle redazioni del 1550 e 1568*, ed. P. Barocchi, voll. 5, Milano-Napoi, 1962.

Zangheri L., *Il parato Farnese dell'Accademia delle Arti del Disegno e la corrispondenza del Cardinale Farnese con i Medici*, in *I Farnese dalla Tuscia alle Corti d'Europa*, proceedings of the international congress (Gradoli 1987), to be published.

# Index of artists

Printed by Electa
by Fantonigrafica, Venice